PENGUIN BOOK

Through England on a Side-Saddle

THROUGH ENGLAND ON A SIDE-SADDLE

Celia
Fiennes

English Journeys

PENGUIN BOOKS

Published by the Penguin Group
Penguin Books Ltd, 80 Strand, London WC2R ORL, England
Penguin Group (USA) Inc., 375 Hudson Street, New York, New York 10014, USA
Penguin Group (Canada), 90 Eglinton Avenue East, Suite 700, Toronto, Ontario, Canada M4P 2Y3
(a division of Pearson Penguin Canada Inc.)
Penguin Ireland, 25 St Stephen's Green, Dublin 2, Ireland
(a division of Penguin Books Ltd)
Penguin Group (Australia), 250 Camberwell Road, Camberwell, Victoria 3124, Australia
(a division of Pearson Australia Group Pty Ltd)
Penguin Books India Pvt Ltd, 11 Community Centre, Panchsheel Park, New Delhi – 110 017, India
Penguin Group (NZ), 67 Apollo Drive, Rosedale, North Shore 0632, New Zealand
(a division of Pearson New Zealand Ltd)
Penguin Books (South Africa) (Pty) Ltd, 24 Sturdee Avenue, Rosebank, Johannesburg 2196, South Africa

Penguin Books Ltd, Registered Offices: 80 Strand, London WC2R ORL, England

www.penguin.com

This selection taken from *The Journeys of Celia Fiennes*, first published by
The Cresset Press, 1947
Published in Penguin Books 2009
1

Set by Rowland Phototypesetting Ltd, Bury St Edmunds, Suffolk
Printed in England by Clays Ltd, St Ives plc

978-0-141-19107-2

www.greenpenguin.co.uk

Mixed Sources
Product group from well-managed
forests and other controlled sources
www.fsc.org Cert no. SA-COC-1592
© 1996 Forest Stewardship Council

Penguin Books is committed to a sustainable future
for our business, our readers and our planet.
The book in your hands is made from paper
certified by the Forest Stewardship Council.

Contents

Note on the Text

The following extracts are taken from Celia Fiennes's journal on her 'Great Journey to Newcastle and to Cornwall' made in 1698. As part of that journey Celia also visited Wolseley, which is where the narrative of this book begins.

From Wolseley Through Cheshire into Wales and Out Again

I tooke my progress northward and went to Newcastle under Line through Stone which was 9 mile, and then to Trentum and passed by a great house of Mr Leveston Gore, and went on the side of a high hill below which the River Trent rann and turn'd its silver streame forward and backward into Ss which looked very pleasant circleing about the fine meadows in their flourishing tyme, bedecked with hay almost ripe and flowers; 6 mile more to Newcastle Underline where is the fine shineing Channell Coale, so the proverb to both the Newcastles of bringing Coales to them is a needless labour, one being famous for this coale thats cloven and makes white ashes, as is this, and the Newcastle on the Tyne is for the sea-coale that cakes and is what is common and famillier to every smith in all villages; I went to this Newcastle in Staffordshire to see the makeing the fine tea-potts cups and saucers of the fine red earth, in imitation and as curious as that which comes from China, but was defeated in my design, they comeing to an end of their clay they made use off for that sort of ware and therefore was remov'd to some other place where they were not settled at their work, so could not see it; therefore I went on to Betely 6 miles farther and went by a ruinated Castle the walls still remaineing called

Healy Castle – this was deep clay way; this town is halfe in Staffordshire and halfe in Cheshire one side of the streete in the one and the other in the latter, so that they often jest on it in travelling one wheele goes in Staffordshire the other wheele in Cheshire; here is a great mer or standing water 2 miles compass great store of good fish, it belongs to one Mr Egerton.

Thence I went to Nantwitch 5 long miles; Nantwitch is a pretty large town and well built, here are the salt springs of which they make salt and many salterns which were a boyling the salt; this is a pretty rich land; you must travell on a Caussey, I went 3 miles on a Caussey through much wood; its from Nantwitch to Chester town 14 long miles the wayes being deep; its much on enclosures and I passed by severall large pooles of waters but what I wonder'd at was that tho' this shire is remarkable for a greate deale of greate Cheeses and Dairys I did not see more than 20 or 30 cowes in a troope feeding, but on enquiry find the custome of the country to joyn their milking together of a whole village and so make their great Cheeses and so it goes round.

West Chester town lies in a bottom and runs a greate length and is pretty big there are 10 Churches; the Cathedrall is large and lofty, the quire well carv'd fine tapistry hangings at the alter, a good organ; the Bishops Pallace is on the right hand of it and the Doctors houses all built of stone, there is a new Hall building which is for the assize and it stands on great stone pillars which is to be the Exchange, which will be very convenient and handsome; the Hall is round, its built of bricke and stone coynes, there are leads all round with battlements and in the middle is a tower; there are ballconies on the side and windows quite round the Cupillow that shews the whole town round; there is another Town Hall a long lofty place and another by the side which is called the Councill Roome both for the Major [Mayor] and Aldermen to meet for the buissinesse of the Corporation; the town is walled all aboute with battlements and a walke all round pav'd with stone; I allmost encompass'd the walls; the streetes are of a greate breadth from the houses, but there is one thing takes much from their appeareing so and from their beauty, for on each side in most places they have made penthouses so broad set on pillars which persons walks under covert, and is made up and down steps under which are ware houses; tho' a penthouse or pallasadoe be convenient and a security from the sun or weather and were it no broader than for two to passe one by the other it would be well and no dissight to the grace of the streetes, but this does darken the streetes and hinder the light of the houses in many places to the streete ward below; indeed in some places were it only before the chiefe persons houses it would be convenient where its flatt and even with the streetes; the town is mostly timber buildings, the trade and con-course of people to it is chiefly from the intercourse it has with Ireland, most take this passage, and also the intercourse with Wales which is parted from it and England by the River Dee, which washes the Castle walls in which they keep their stores – but nothing fine in it – the walls and towers seemes in good repaire; at the end of the town just by the Castle you crosse over a very large and long Bridge over the River Dee which has the tyde comes up much beyond the town, its 7 mile off that it falls into the sea but its very broad below the town, when at high tyde is like a very broad sea; there they have a little dock and build shipps of 200 tunn I saw some on the stocks.

Cross this river by this bridge enters Flintshire and so crossed over the marshes, which is hazardous to strangers, therefore Mr William Allen (which was the Major of Chester that tyme and gave me a very civil treate being an acquaintance of my Brother Sir Edmund Harrison) so order'd his son and another gentleman to ride with me to direct to Harding [Hawarden] which was 5 mile; just by that was a very fine new built house of brick and in the exact forme of the London architecture which was this Mr Majors house and good gardens.

Att Harding, where was my Relation, Dr Percivalls wife, who was Minister of that place; his parish was 8 miles in extent and 2 lordships in it and the ruines of two great Castles in it remaines, its good rich land here much on enclosures and woods; in a tarresse walke in my Relations garden I could very plainly see Chester and the River Dee with all its washes over the marsh ground which look'd very finely; here are sands which makes it very difficult for strangers to passe without a guide; from thence my Relation carry'd me to Holly Well and pass'd thro' Flint town which is the shire town, 5 mile from Harding; its a very ragged place many villages in England are better, the houses all thatched and stone walls but so decay'd that in many places ready to tumble down; there was a Town Hall such a one as it was; it was at a Session tyme when I was there which shew'd it at its prime;

there is a Castle which still remaines with its towers built of stone, its down to the water side; from thence to Holy well is 3 mile mostly by the water side which is reckon'd the sea – here I went just in sight of High Lake where were many shipps rideing along that harbour.

St Winfreds Well is built over with stone on pillars like a tryumphall arch or tower on the gates of a Church; there is a pavement of stone within ground 3 sides of the Well which is joyn'd on the fourth side by a great arch of stone which lies over the water that runs off from the Well, its many springs which bubbles up very fast and lookes cleane in a compass which is 8 square walled in with stone; in the bottom which you see as clear as Chrystall are 9 stones layd in an oval on which are dropps of red coullour some almost quite covering the top of the stone, which is pretended to be the blood of this holy saint whose head was struck off here, and so where her body laid this spring burst forth and remaines till now, a very rapid current, which runs off from this Well under a barre by which there are stone stepps for the persons to descend which will bathe themselves in the Well; and so they walke along the streame to the other end and then come out, but there is nothing to shelter them but are exposed to all the Company that are walking about the Well and to the little houses and part of the streete which runs along by it; but the Religeuse are not to mind that; it seemes the Saint they do honour to in this place must beare them out in all things, they tell of many lameness's and aches and distempers which are cured by it; its a cold water and cleare and runs off very quick so that it would be a pleasant refreshment in the sumer to

Celia Fiennes

washe ones self in it, but its shallow not up to the waste so its not easye to dive and washe in; but I thinke I could not have been persuaded to have gone in unless might have had curtains to have drawn about some part of it to have shelter'd from the streete, for the wett garments are no covering to the body; but there I saw abundance of the devout papists on their knees all round the Well; poor people are deluded into an ignorant blind zeale and to be pity'd by us that have the advantage of knowing better and ought to be better; there is some small stones of a reddish coullour in the Well said to be some of St Winifreds blood also, which the poore people take out and bring to the strangers for curiosity and relicts, and also moss about the bancks full of great virtue for every thing – but its a certaine gaine to the poore people, every one gives them something for bringing them moss and the stones, but least they should in length of tyme be quite gather'd up they take care to replenish it dayly from some mossy hill and so stick it along the sides of the Well – there is good streames runs from it and by meanes of steepe descent runs down and turns mills; they come also to drinke of the water which they take up in the first square which is walled round and where the springs rise, and they say its of wonder full operation; the taste to me was but like good spring water which with wine and sugar and leamons might make a pleasant draught after walking amongst those shady trees of which there is a great many and some straight and tall like a grove but not very uniforme, but a sort of iregular rows.

From thence I went back to Harding which is 8 very

long miles; at Holly Well they speake Welsh, the inhabitants go barefoote and bare leg'd a nasty sort of people, their meate is very small here, mutton is noe bigger than little lamb, what of it there is was sweete; their wine good being neare the sea side and are well provided with fish, very good salmon and eeles and other fish I had at Harding.

This shire is improperly called Flintshire there being noe flints in all the country; there are great coale pitts of the Channell Coale thats cloven huge great pieces, they have great wheeles that are turned with horses that draw up the water and so draine the Mines which would else be overflowed so as they could not dig the coale; they have also engines that draw up their coale in sort of baskets like hand barrows which they wind up like a bucket in a well, for their mines are dug down through a sort of well and sometymes its pretty low before they come to the coales; it makes the road unsafe because of the coale pitts and also from the slough and quick sands all here about being mostly near the bancks of the water.

In this country are quarrys of stone, copper and iron mines and salt hills, its a hilly place very steep descents great many very high hills, but I went not so farre as Pen ma mower but cross'd the River Dee haveing first went two mile by these coale mines at least 10 in a place; its a thing which holds neer 2 bushell that is their basket they draw up which is bought for 6 pence.

I forded over the Dee when the tide was out all upon the sands at least a mile which was as smooth as a die being a few hours left of the flood; the sands are here soe loose that the tydes does move them from one place to another at every flood, that the same place one used to foard a month or two before is not to be pass'd now, for as it brings the sands in heaps to one place so it leaves others in deep holes, which are cover'd with water, and loose sand that would swallow up a horse or carriages, so I had two Guides to conduct me over; the carriages which are used to it and pass continually at the ebbs of water observes the drift of sands and so escape the danger; it was at least a mile I went on the sands before I came to the middle of the channell which was pretty deep, and with such a current or tyde which was falling out to sea together with the wind the horses feete could scarce stand against it, but it was but narrow just the deep part of the channell and so soone over; when the tyde is fully out they frequently ford in many places which they marke as the sands fall, and can go near 9 or 10 mile over the sands from Chester to Burton or to Flint town almost; but many persons that have known the foards well, that have come a year or half a year after, if they venture on their former knowledge have been overwhelm'd in the ditches made by the sands, which is deep enough to swallow up a coach or waggon; but they convey their coales from Wales and any other things by waggon when the tyde is out to Chester and other parts.

From Burton which was on the side of England the shore I went to the ferry 9 miles to the River Meresy, another great river indeed much broader and a perfect sea for 20 mile or more; it comes out of Lancashire from Warrington and both this and the Dee empts themselves into the sea almost together a few leagues from Leverpoole which poole is form'd by a poynt of land that runs almost round the entrance from the sea, being narrow and hazardous to strangers to saile in in the winter, the mouth of the river by reason of the sands and rocks is a gate to the river; this I ferry'd over and was an hour and halfe in the passage, its of great bredth and at low water is so deep and salt as the sea almost, tho' it does not cast so green a hew on the water as the sea, but else the waves toss and the rocks great all round it and is as dangerous as the sea; its in a sort of Hoy that I ferried over and my horses, the boate would have held 100 people.

Lancashire and the Lake District

Leverpool which is in Lancashire is built just on the river Mersy, mostly new built houses of brick and stone after the London fashion; the first original was a few fishermens houses and now is grown to a large fine town and but a parish and one Church, tho' there be 24 streetes in it; there is indeed a little Chappell and there are a great many Dessenters in the town; its a very rich trading town the houses of brick and stone built high and even, that a streete quite through lookes very handsome, the streetes well pitched; there are abundance of persons you see very well dress'd and of good fashion; the streetes are faire and long, its London in miniature as much as ever I saw any thing; there is a very pretty Exchange stands on 8 pillars besides the corners which are each treble pillars all of stone and its railed in over which is a very handsome Town Hall; over all is a tower and cupillow thats so high that from thence one has the whole view of the town and the country round; in a clear day you may see the Isle of Man – which also was in view from out of Wales at Harding on the high tarrass walke in my Cos'n Percivalls garden.

Thence to Prescote 7 very long miles but pretty good way mostly lanes; there I passed by Mosel [Knowsley], the Earle of Darbys house which looked very nobly with many towers and balls on them; it stands amongst tall trees and lookes like a pleasant grove all about it; its an old house runs a large compass of ground; the town of Prescote stands on a high hill, a very pretty neate market town a large market place and broad streetes well pitch'd.

Thence to Wiggon 7 long miles more, mostly in lanes and some hollow wayes, and some pretty deep stony way so forced us upon the high Causey many [times]; but some of the way was good which I went pretty fast, and yet by reason of the tediousness of the miles for length I was 5 hours going that 14 mile, I could have gone 30 mile about London in the time; there was pretty much woods and lanes through which I pass'd, and pass'd by a mer or lake of water; there are many of these here about; but not going through Ormskerk I avoided going by the famous Mer call'd Martin Mer that as the proverb sayes has parted many a man and his mare indeed; it being neare evening and not getting a Guide I was a little afraid to go that way it being very hazardous for Strangers to pass by it; some part of that mer one Mr Fleetewood has been at the expence to draine so as to be able to use the ground for tillage, having by trenches and floodgates with banks shutt out the waters that still kept it a marsh and moorish ground, but it was a very great charge; however it shews by industry and some expence if Gentlemen would set about it most of the waste ground, thats now a fenny moor and mostly water, might be rendred usefull and in a few yeares answere the first great charge on it;

Wiggons is another pretty market town built of stone and brick; here it is that the fine Channell Coales are in perfection, burns as light as a candle – set the coales together with some fire and it shall give a snap and burn up light – of this coale they make saltcellars standishes and many boxes and things which are sent about for Curiositys and sold in London and are often offer'd in the exchanges in company with white or black marble, and most people deceived by them which have not been in those countrys and know it, but such persons discover it and will call for a candle to trye them wheather marble or coale; its very finely pollish'd and lookes much like jett or ebany wood for which one might easily take it when in boxes etc.; I bought some of them for Curiosity sake.

2 mile off Wigon towards Warrington – which was some of my way back againe but for the Curiosity's sake I did – is the Burning Well which burns like brandy; its a little sorry hole in one of the grounds 100 yards from the road that comes from Warrington to Wiggon, just by a hedge or banck, its full of dirt and mud almost but the water continually bubbles up as if it were a pott boyling which is the spring or severall springs in that place, nevertheless I felt the water and it was a Cold Spring; the man which shewed it me with a dish tooke out a good quantety of the water and threw away and then, with a piece of rush he lighted by a candle that he brought in a lanthorne, he set the water in the well on fire, and it burn'd blewish just like spirits and continued a good while, but by reason of the great raines that fell the night before the spring was weaker and had not thrown off the raine water, otherwise it used to flame all over the well a good height now it burnt weaker; however at last the wind blew out the mans candle, and

he severall tymes lighted the bitt of rush or splinter of
wood by the flame that burnt in the well; this is a little
unacountable I apprehend its a sort of an unctious matter
in the earth and soe through its veines the springs run
which causes it so to burn, for I observ'd when they dug
into the banck and opened the sort of clay or mudd it
burnt fiercer and more.

From the Well I returned againe to Wiggon two mile
and thence to Preston, and passed by Sir John Bradshaws
house which stood on the declineing of a hill in the midst
of a fine grove of trees; severall fine walkes and rows of
trees thereabout; just in the road on the banck whereon
the hedge stood was errected a high stone pillar carv'd
and a ball on the top with an inscription cutt on it
shewing the cause of it, being the Monument of an
officer that in a fight just there – his horse takeing the
hedge and ditch on some distaste he tooke at the gunns
and smoake – flung out his sword out of the scabbard
and flung his Master down on the poynt of it which run
him through that he dyed and lyes buried on the spott.

Preston is reckon'd but 12 miles from Wiggon but
they exceed in length by farre those that I thought long
the day before from Leverpoole; its true to avoid the
many mers and marshy places it was a great compass I
tooke and passed down and up very steep hills and this
way was good gravel way; but passing by many very
large arches that were only single ones but as large as
two great gateways and the water I went through that
ran under them was so shallow notwithstanding these
were extream high arches, I enquired the meaneing and
was inform'd that on great raines those brookes would

be swell'd to so great a heigth that unless those arches were so high noe passing while it were so; they are but narrow bridges for foote or horse and at such flouds they are forced in many places to boate it till they come to those arches on the great bridges which are across their great rivers: this happens sometymes on sudden great showers for a day or two in the summer, but the winter is often or mostly soe that there is deep waters so as not easily cross'd; but once in 3 or 4 yeares there is some of those very greate floods I mention'd before that they are forced to boate from bridge to bridge which is little enough then to secure them; I passed by at least half a dozen of these high single arches besides severall great Stone Bridges of 4 or 6 arches which are very high also over their greatest rivers.

Preston stands on a hill is a very good market town, Satterday is their market which day I was there and saw it was provided with all sorts of things leather corn coales butter cheese and fruite and garden things; there is a very spacious Market place and pretty Church and severall good houses; at the entrance of the town was a very good house which was a Lawyers, all stone work 5 windows in the front and high built according to the eastern building neer London, the ascent to the houes was 14 or 15 stone stepps large and a handsome court with open iron pallasadoes in the gate and on each side the whole breadth of the house, which discover'd the gardens on each side of the house neately kept flowers and greens; there was also many steps up to the house from the court it was a compleate building; there was 2 or 3 more such houses in the town and indeed the generallity of the buildings especially in 2 or 3 of the great streetes were very handsome, better than is most country towns, and the streets spacious and well pitch'd.

I was about 4 houres going this twelve mile and could have gone 20 in the tyme in most countrys, nay by the people of those parts this twelve mile is as long and as much tyme taken up in going it as to go from thence to Lancaster which is 20 mile; and I can confirme this by my own experience for I went to Gascoyne [Garstang] which is 10 miles and halfe way to Lancaster in two houres, where I baited, and here it was I was first presented with the Clap bread which is much talked off made all of oates; I was surpris'd when the cloth was laid they brought a great basket such as one uses to undress children with, and set on the table full of thinn waffers as big as pancackes and drye that they easily breake into shivers, but coming to dinner found it to be the only thing I must eate for bread; the taste of oate bread is pleasant enough and where its well made is very acceptable, but for the most part its scarce baked and full of drye flower on the outside; the description of how its made ought to come in here but I reserve it to the place I saw it made at the best way.

As I come to this place which was much over Downs or a Race ground I came along by some of the old Picts walls the ruines of which here and there remaines in many parts of the country; Gascoyn is a little market town, one Church in it which is a mile off from the town, and the parish is 8 miles long which discourag'd me in staying there being Satturday night and so pressed

on to Lancaster; I perceive most of the parishes are a
great tract of land and very large and also as beneficial,
for all over Lancastershire the revenues of the parsonages
are considerable, 2 and 300£, 500 and 800£ apiece; the
parson at Leverpoole has 1100£ a yeare and its frequent
every where 3 or 400£.

Thence to Lancaster town 10 mile more which I easily
reached in 2 hours and a halfe or 3 hours, I passed through
abundance of villages, almost at the end of every mile,
mostly all along lanes being an enclosed country; they
have one good thing in most parts off this principality
(or County Palatine its rather called) that at all cross
wayes there are Posts with Hands pointing to each road
with the names of the great town or market towns that
it leads to, which does make up for the length of the
miles that strangers may not loose their road and have
it to goe back againe; you have a great divertion on this
road haveing a pleasing prospect of the countrys a great
distance round and see it full of inclosures and some
woods; three miles off the town you see it very plaine
and the sea even the main ocean in one place an arm of
it comes up within 2 mile of the town; the River Lieue
[Lune] runs by the town and so into the sea.

The situation of Lancaster town is very good, the
Church neately built of stone, the Castle which is just
by, both on a very great ascent from the rest of the town
and so is in open view, the town and river lying round
it beneath; on the Castle tower walking quite round by
the battlements I saw the whole town and river at a
view, which runs almost quite round and returns againe
by the town, and saw the sea beyond and the great high

hills beyond that part of the sea which are in Wales, and also into Westmoreland to the great hills there call'd Furness Fells or Hills being a string of vast high hills together; also into Cumberland to the great hill called Black Comb Hill whence they digg their black lead and no where else, but they open the mine but once in severall yeares; I also saw into Yorkshire; there is lead copper gold and silver in some of those hills and marble and christall also.

Lancaster town is old and much decay'd; there has been a monastery, the walls of part of it remaine and some of the carv'd stones and figures, there is in it a good garden and a pond in it with a little isleand on which an apple tree grows, a Jenitin, and strawberys all round its rootes and the banks of the little isle; there are 2 pretty wells and a vault that leads a great way under ground up as farre as the Castle which is a good distance; in the river there are great wires or falls of water made for salmon fishing, where they hang their nets and catch great quantety's of fish, which is neare the bridge; the town seems not to be much in trade as some others, but the great store of fish makes them live plentifully as also the great plenty of all provisions; the streetes are some of them well pitch'd and of a good size; when I came into the town the stones were so slippery crossing some channells that my horse was quite down on his nose but did at length recover himself and so I was not thrown off or injured, which I desire to bless God for as for the many preservations I mett with – I cannot say the town seemes a lazy town and there are trades of all sorts, there is a large meeteing-house but their Minister was but a

mean preacher: there are 2 Churches in the town which
are pretty near each other.

Thence I went to Kendall in Westmoreland over
steepe stony hills all like rocks 6 miles to one Lady
Middleton; and by some Gentlemen which were travelling that way that was their acquantaince had the advantage of going through her parke and saved the going
round a bad stony passage; it was very pleasant under
the shade of the tall trees; it was an old timber house but
the family being from home we had a free passage
through on to the road againe much of which was stony
and steep far worse than the Peake in Darbyshire; this
Lady Middleton was a papist and I believe the Gentlemen
that was travelling were too; in this park is the 3 Brother
tree which a little from the root measures 13 yards
circumference; thence to Kendall ten mile more, most
of the way was in lanes when I was out of the stony hills,
and then into inclosed lands; here in 6 mile to the town
you have very rich good land enclosed, little round green
hills flourishing with corn and grass as green and fresh
being in the prime season in July; there is not much
woods but only the hedge rows round the grounds which
looks very fine; in these Northern Countyes they have
only the summer graine as barley oates peas beans and
lentils noe wheate or rhye, for they are so cold and late
in their yeare they cannot venture at that sort of tillage,
so have none but what they are supply'd out of other
countys adjacent; the land seemes here in many places
very fertile; they have much rhye in Lancashire Yorkshire and Stafford and Shropshire and so Herriford and
Worcestershire which I found very troublesome in my

journeys, for they would not own they had any such thing in their bread but it so disagrees with me as allwayes to make me sick, which I found by its effects when ever I met with any tho' I did not discern it by the taste; in Suffolke and Norfolke I also met with it – but in these parts its altogether the oatbread.

Kendall is a town built all of stone, one very broad streete in which is the Market Crosse, its a goode tradeing town mostly famed for the cottons; Kendall Cotton is used for blanckets and the Scotts use them for their plodds [plaids] and there is much made here and also linsiwoolseys and a great deale of leather tann'd here and all sorts of commodityes twice a weeke is the market furnished with all sorts of things.

The River Can which gives name to the town is pretty large but full of rocks and stones that makes shelves and falls in the water, its stor'd with plenty of good fish and there are great falls of water partly naturall and added to by putting more stones in manner of wyers [weirs] at which they catch salmon when they leape with speares; the roareing of the water at these places sometymes does foretell wet weather, they do observe when the water roares most in the fall on the northside it will be faire, if on the southside of the town it will be wet; some of them are falls as high as a house – the same observation is at Lancaster at the wires [weirs] where they catch salmon, against storms or raines it will be turbulent and rore as may be heard into the town – there are 3 or 4 good houses in the town, the rest are like good traders houses very neate and tight, the streetes are all pitch'd which is extreame easy to be repair'd for the whole country is like one entire rock or pitching almost all the roads.

At the Kings Arms one Mrs Rowlandson she does pott up the charr fish the best of any in the country, I was curious to have some and so bespoke some of her, and also was as curious to see the great water which is the only place that fish is to be found in, and so went from Kendall to Bondor [Bowness] 6 miles thro' narrow lanes, but the lands in the inclosures are rich; but here can be noe carriages but very narrow ones like little wheel-barrows that with a horse they convey their fewell and all things else; they also use horses on which they have a sort of pannyers some close some open that they strew full of hay turff and lime and dung and every thing they would use, and the reason is plaine from the narrowness of the lanes: where is good lands they will loose as little as they can and where its hilly and stoney no other carriages can pass, so they use these horse carriages; abundance of horses I see all about Kendall streetes with their burdens.

This Kendall is the biggest town and much in the heart of Westmoreland but Appleby 10 mile off is the shire town where the session and assizes are held and is 7 miles to this great Lake Wiandermer great standing water, which is 10 mile long and near halfe a mile over in some places; it has many little hills or isles in it, one of a great bigness of 30 acres of ground on which is a house, the Gentleman that is Lord of the Manour lives in it Sir Christopher Phillips he has a great command of the water, and of the villages thereabout and many privi-leges, he makes a Major or Bailiff of the place during life;

its but a small mean place, Mr Majors was the best entertaining house where I was; the Isle did not looke to be so bigg at the shore but takeing boate I went on it and found it as large and very good barley and oates and grass; the water is very cleer and full of good fish, but the Charr fish being out of season could not easily be taken so I saw none alive, but of other fish I had a very good supper; the season of the Charrfish is between Michaelmas and Christmas, at that tyme I have had of them which they pott with sweete spices, they are as big as a small trout rather slenderer and the skinn full of spotts some redish, and part of the whole skinn and the finn and taile is red like the finns of a perch, and the inside flesh looks as red as any salmon; if they are in season their taste is very rich and fatt tho' not so strong or clogging as the lamprys are, but its as fatt and rich a food.

This great water seemes to flow and wave about with the wind or in one motion but it does not ebb and flow like the sea with the tyde, neither does it run so as to be perceivable tho' at the end of it a little rivulet trills from it into the sea, but it seemes to be a standing lake encompass'd with vast high hills that are perfect rocks and barren ground of a vast height from which many little springs out of the rock does bubble up and descend down and fall into this water; notwithstanding great raines the water does not seem much encreased, tho' it must be so, then it does draine off more at the end of the Lake; these hills which they call Furness Fells a long row continued some miles and some of them are call'd Donum Fells and soe from the places they adjoyne to are named, but they hold the whole length of the water which is 10 mile; they have some parts of them that has wayes that they can by degrees in a compass ascend them and so they go onward in the countrys; they are ferried over the Lake when they go to market; on the other side over those fels there is a sort of stones like rubbish or broken pieces of stones which lies about a quarry that lies all in the bottom of the water; where its so shallow as at the shores it is and very cleer you see the bottom, between these stones are weeds which grows up that I had some taken up, just like sampyer and I have a fancy its a sort of sampire that indeed is gather'd in the rocks by the sea and water, and this grows in the water but it resembles it in coullour figure and the taste not much unlike, it was somewhat waterish; there was also fine moss growing in the bottom of the water.

Here it was I saw the oat Clap bread made: they mix their flour with water so soft as to rowle it in their hands into a ball, and then they have a board made round and something hollow in the middle riseing by degrees all round to the edge a little higher, but so little as one would take it to be only a board warp'd, this is to cast out the cake thinn and so they clap it round and drive it to the edge in a due proportion till drove as thinn as a paper, and still they clap it and drive it round, and then they have a plaite of iron same size with their clap board and so shove off the cake on it and so set it on coales and bake it; when enough on one side they slide it off and put the other side; if their iron plaite is smooth and they take care their coales or embers are not too hot but just to make it looke yellow, it will bake and be as crisp and pleasant to eate as any thing you can imagine; but as we say of all sorts of bread there is a vast deale of difference in what is housewifely made and what is ill made, so this if its well mixed and rowled up and but a little flour on the outside which will drye on and make it mealy is a very good sort of food; this is the sort of bread they use in all these countrys, and in Scotland they breake into their milk or broth or else sup that up and bite of their bread between while, they spread butter on it and eate it with their meate; they have no other sort of bread unless at market towns and that is scarce to be had unless the market dayes, soe they make their cake and eate it presently for its not so good if 2 or 3 dayes old; it made me reflect on the description made in scripture of their kneeding cakes and bakeing them on the hearth when ever they had Company come to their houses, and I cannot but thinke it was after this maner they made their bread in the old tymes especially those Eastern Countryes where their bread might be soone dry'd and spoil'd.

Their little carts I was speakeing of they use here about, the wheeles are fast'ned to the axletree and so turn altogether, they hold not above what our wheele barrows would carry at three or four tymes, which the girles and boys and women does go about with, drawn by one horse to carry any thing they want; here is a great deal of good grass and summer corn and pastures its rich land in the bottoms, as one may call them considering the vast hills above them on all sides, yet they contain a number of lesser hills one below another, so that tho' at one looke you think it but a little land every body has, yet it being so full of hills its many acres which if at length in a plain would extend a vast way; I was about a quarter of an hour in the boate before I reach'd the island which is in the midst of the water so by that you may guesse at the breadth of the water in the whole; they ferry man and horse over it, its sometymes perfectly calme.

Thence I rode almost all the waye in sight of this great water; some tymes I lost it by reason of the great hills interposeing and so a continu'd up hill and down hill and that pretty steep even when I was in that they called bottoms, which are very rich good grounds, and so I gained by degrees from lower to higher hills which I allwayes went up and down before I came to another hill; at last I attained to the side of one of these hills or fells of rocks which I passed on the side much about the middle; for looking down to the bottom it was at least a mile all full of those lesser hills and inclosures, so looking upward I was as farre from the top which was all rocks and something more barren tho' there was some trees and woods growing in the rocks and hanging over all down the brow of some of the hills; from these great fells there are severall springs out of the rock that trickle down their sides, and as they meete with stones and rocks in the way when something obstructs their passage and so they come with more violence that gives a pleaseing sound and murmuring noise; these descend by degrees, at last fall into the low grounds and fructifye it which makes the land soe fruit full in the valleys; and upon those very high fells or rocky hills its (tho') soe

high and yet a moorish sort off ground whence they digg
abundance of peat which they use for their fewell, being
in many places a barren ground yielding noe wood, etc.;
I rode in sight of this Winander Water as I was saying
up and down above 7 mile; afterwards as I was ascending
another of those barren fells – which tho' I at last was
not halfe way up, yet was an hour going it up and down,
on the other side going only on the side of it about the
middle of it, but it was of such a height as to shew one
a great deale of the Country when it happens to be
between those hills, else those interposeing hinders any
sight but of the clouds – I see a good way behind me
another of those waters or mers but not very bigge;
these great hills are so full of loose stones and shelves of
rocks that its very unsafe to ride them down.

There is good marble amongst those rocks: as I walked
down at this place I was walled on both sides by those
inaccessible high rocky barren hills which hangs over
ones head in some places and appear very terrible; and
from them springs many little currents of water from
the sides and clefts which trickle down to some lower
part where it runs swiftly over the stones and shelves in
the way, which makes a pleasant rush and murmuring
noise and like a snow ball is encreased by each spring
trickling down on either side of those hills, and so
descends into the bottoms which are a moorish ground
in which in many places the waters stand, and so forme
some of those Lakes as it did here, the confluence of all
these little springs being gathered together in this Lake
which was soe deep as the current of water that passed
through it was scarce to be perceived till one came to

the farther end, from whence it run a good little river and pretty quick, over which many bridges are laid.

Here I came to villages of sad little hutts made up of drye walls, only stones piled together and the roofs of same slatt; there seemed to be little or noe tunnells for their chimneys and have no morter or plaister within or without; for the most part I tooke them at first sight for a sort of houses or barns to fodder cattle in, not thinking them to be dwelling houses, they being scattering houses here one there another, in some places there may be 20 or 30 together, and the Churches the same; it must needs be very cold dwellings but it shews something of the lazyness of the people; indeed here and there there was a house plaister'd, but there is sad entertainment, that sort of clap bread and butter and cheese and a cup of beer all one can have, they are 8 mile from a market town and their miles are tedious to go both for illness of way and length of the miles.

They reckon it but 8 mile from the place I was at the night before but I was 3 or 4 hours at least going it; here I found a very good smith to shooe the horses, for these stony hills and wayes pulls off a shooe presently and wears them as thinn that it was a constant charge to shooe my horses every 2 or 3 days; but this smith did shooe them so well and so good shooes that they held some of the shooes 6 weeks; the stonyness of the wayes all here about teaches them the art off making good shooes and setting them on fast.

Here I cross'd one of the stone bridges that was pretty large which entred me into Cumberlandshire: this river together with the additional springs continually running into it all the way from those vaste precipices comes into a low place and form a broad water which is very cleer and reaches 7 mile in length, Ules water it's called, such another water as that of Wiander mer only that reaches 10 mile in length from Ambleside to the sea, and this is but 7 such miles long; its full of such sort of stones and slatts in the bottom as the other, neer the brimm where its shallowe you see it cleer to the bottom; this is secured on each side by such formidable heights as those rocky fells in same manner as the other was; I rode the whole length of this water by its side sometyme a little higher upon the side of the hill and sometyme just by the shore and for 3 or 4 miles I rode through a fine forest or parke where was deer skipping about and haires, which by meanes of a good Greyhound I had a little Course, but we being strangers could not so fast pursue it in the grounds full of hillocks and furse and soe she escaped us.

I observed the boundaries of all these great waters, which are a sort of deep lakes or kind of standing waters, are those sort of barren rocky hills which are so vastly high; I call this a standing water as the other because its not like other great rivers as the Trent Severne Hull or Thames etc. to appear to run with a streame or current, but only as it rowles from side to side like waves as the wind moves it; its true at the end of this being a low fall of ground it runs off in a little streame; there is exceeding good fish here and all sorts of provision at the market towns; their market town was Peroth [Penrith] 10 long miles, a mile or two beyond this Ulls water; Tuesday is the market day which was the day I came thither, its a long way for the market people to goe but they and their horses are used to it and go with much more facility than strangers; at the end of this Ulls water is a fine round hill look'd as green and full of wood, very pleasant with grass and corne very fruitefull, and hereabout we leave those desart and barren rocky hills, not that they are limitted to Westmorland only, for had I gone farther to the left hand on into Cumberland I should have found more such and they tell me farr worse for height and stonynesse about White haven side and Cockermouth, so that tho' both the County's have very good land and fruitfull, so they equally partake of the bad, tho' indeed Westmorland takes it name from its abounding in moorish ground yet Cumberland has its share, and more of the hilly stony part; indeed I did observe those grounds were usually neighbours to each other, the rocks abounding in springs which distilling it self on lower ground if of a spungy soile made it marshy or lakes, and in many places very fruitfull in summer graine and grasse, but the northerly winds blow cold so long on them that they never attempt sowing their land with wheate or rhye.

The stones and slatt about Peroth look'd so red that at my entrance into the town thought its buildings were all of brick, but after found it to be the coullour of the stone which I saw in the Quarrys look very red, their slatt is the same which cover their houses; its a pretty large town a good market for cloth that they spinn in the country, hempe and also woollen; its a great market for all sorts of cattle meate corne etc.

Here are two rivers one called the Emount which parts Cumberland and Westmorland which bridge I should have passed over had I come the direct roade

from Kendall to Peroth, but strikeing off to Ambleside
to Wiandermer I came another end of the town; in this
river are greate falls of waters call'd cataracts by reason
of the rock and shelves in it which makes a great noise,
which is heard more against foul weather into the town
tho' the bridge be halfe a mile out of the town; the other
river is called Louder [Lowther] which gives name to
Lord Landsdowns house call'd Louder-hall which is four
mile from Peroth; I went to it through fine woods, the
front is just faceing the great road from Kendall and
lookes very nobly, with severall rows of trees which
leads to large iron gates, open barres, into the stable yard
which is a fine building on the one side of the house
very uniform, and just against it is such another row of
buildings the other side of the house like two wings
which is the offices; its built each like a fine house jutting
out at each end and the middle is with pillars white and
carvings like the entrance of a building, these are just
equal and alike and encompass the two sides of the
first court which enters with large iron gates and iron
palasadoes in the breadth, and then there is an ascent of
15 stone steps turned round very large and on the top
large iron gates and same pallisad of iron betweene stone
pillars, which runs the breadth of the front; this court is
with paved walks of broad stone one broad one to the
house, the other of same breadth runs acrosse to the
stables and offices and so there is 4 large squares of grass
in which there is a large statue of stone in the midst of
each and 4 little Cupids or little boys in each corner of
the 4 squares; then one ascends severall more steps to
another little court with open iron railes and this is

divided into severall grass plotts by paved walks of stone
to the severall doores, some of which are straight others
slope, the grass plotts being seven, and in each a statue,
the middlemost is taller than the rest; this is just the front
of the house where you enter a porch with pillars of
lime stone but the house is the red sort of stone of the
country.

Below-staires you enter a space that leads severall
wayes to all the offices and on one side is a large parlour
which lookes out on these green plotts with images; the
staircase very well wanscoated and carv'd at the top; you
are landed into a noble hall very lofty, the top and sides
are exquisitely painted by the best hand in England which
did the painting at Windsor; the top is the Gods and
Goddesses that are sitting at some great feast and a great
tribunal before them, each corner is the Seasons of the
yeare with the variety of weather, raines and rainbows
stormy winds sun shine snow and frost with multitudes
of other fancyes and varietyes in painting, and looks very
natural – it cost 500£ that roome alone; thence into a
dineing room and drawing-roome well wanscoated of
oake large pannells plaine no frettworks nor carvings or
glass work only in chimney pieces; 3 handsome chambers, one scarlet cloth strip'd and very fashionably made
up the hangings the same, another flower'd damaske
lined with fine Indian embroidery, the third roome had
a blew satten bed embroider'd, in this roome was very
fine orris hangings in which was much silk and gold and
silver; a little roome by in which was a green and white
damaske canopy bed which was hung with some of the
same hangings – being made for the Duke of Lortherdale

and had his armes in many places, by his dying were sold to Lord Landsdon, they containe a Scottish story and garb of the 4 quarters of the yeare; the roomes are all well pitch'd and well finish'd and many good pictures of the family and severall good fancy's of humane and animals; a good gallery so adorn'd which leads to a closet that looks into the Chappell, all things very neat tho' nothing extraordinary besides the hall painting; the chimney pieces are of a dark coulloured marble which is taken out of the ground just by, its well polish'd, there was some few white marble vein'd but that is not dug out of this country.

The house is a flatt rooffe and stands amidst a wood of rows of trees which with these statues and those in two gardens on each side (which for their walks and plantations is not finish'd but full of statues) which with the house is so well contrived to be seen at one view; the Lady Landsdown sent and treated me with a breakfast, cold things and sweetemeates all serv'd in plaite, but it was so early in the morning that she being indisposed was not up.

So I returned back 4 mile to Peroth and came in sight of severall genteele seates or Gentlemens houses, and came by a round green spott of a large circumfference which they keep cut round with a banke round it like a bench its story is that it was the table a great Giant 6 yards tall used to dine at and there entertained another of nine yards tall which he afterwards killed; there is the length in the Church yard how farre he could leape a great many yards; there was also on the Church at Peroth a fine Clock which had severall motions, there was the starrs and signes there was the encrease and changes of the moone by a darke and golden side of a little globe.

A mile from Peroth in a low bottom a moorish place stands Great Mag and her Sisters, the story is that these soliciting her to an unlawfull love by an enchantment are turned with her into stone; the stone in the middle which is called Mag is much bigger and have some forme like a statue or figure of a body but the rest are but soe many craggy stones, but they affirme they cannot be counted twice alike as is the story of Stonidge [Stonehenge], but the number of these are not above 30; however what the first design of placeing them there either as a marke of that sort of moorish ground or what else, the thing is not so wonderfull as that of Stonidge, because there is noe such sort of stone in 20 miles off those downs and how they of so vast a bulk and weight should be brought thither, whereas all this country abounds with quarrys of stone and its mostly rocks.

The wayes from thence to Carlisle over much heath where they have many stone quarrys and cut much peate and turff, which is their chief fuel; its reckon'd but 16 mile from Peroth to Carlisle but they are pretty long, besides my going out of the way above 3 or 4 mile, which made it 20; they were very long and I was a great while rideing it; you pass by the little hutts and hovels the poor live in like barnes some have them daub'd with mud-wall others drye walls.

Carlisle stands in view at least 4 mile distant; the town is walled in and all built of stone, the Cathedrall stands high and very eminent to be seen above the town; you enter over the bridge and double gates which are iron-grates and lined with a case of doores of thick timber; there are 3 gates to the town one called the English gate at which I entred, the other the Irish which leads on to White haven and Cokermouth the other the Scottish gate through which I went into Scotland; the walls of the town and battlements and towers are in very good repaire and looks well; the Cathedrall all built of stone which looked stately but nothing Curious; there was some few houses as the Deans and Treasurer and some of the Doctors houses walled in with little gardens their fronts looked gracefully, else I saw no house except the present Majors house of brick and stone, and one house which was the Chancellors built of stone very lofty 5 good sarshe windows in the front, and this within a stone wall'd garden well kept and iron gates to discover it to view with stone pillars; the streetes are very broad and handsome well pitch'd.

I walked round the walls and saw the river, which twists and turns it self round the grounds, called the Emount which at 3 or 4 miles off is flow'd by the sea; the other river is the Essex which is very broad and ebbs and flows about a mile or two off; there remaines only some of the walls and ruines of the Castle which does shew it to have been a very strong town formerly; the walls are of a prodigious thickness and vast great stones, its moated round and with draw bridges; there is a large Market place with a good Cross and Hall and is well supply'd as I am inform'd with provision at easye rates, but my Landlady notwithstanding ran me up the largest reckoning for allmost nothing; it was the dearest lodging I met with and she pretended she could get me nothing else, so for 2 joynts of mutton and a pinte of wine and bread and beer I had a 12 shilling reckoning; but since, I find tho' I was in the biggest house in town I was in the worst accomodation, and so found it, and a young giddy Landlady that could only dress fine and entertain the soldiers.

Along the Border to Newcastle

From hence I tooke a Guide the next day and so went
for Scotland and rode 3 or 4 mile by the side of this River
Emount which is full of very good fish; I rode sometymes
on a high ridge over a hill sometymes on the sands, it
turning and winding about, that I went almost all the
way by it and saw them with boates fishing for salmon
and troute which made my journey very pleasant; leav-
ing this river I came to the Essex which is very broad
and hazardous to crosse even when the tyde is out, by
which it leaves a broad sand on each side which in some
places is unsafe – made me take a good Guide which
carry'd me aboute and a crosse some part of it here and
some part in another place, it being deep in the channell
where I did crosse which was in sight of the mouth of
the river that runs into the sea; on the sand before the
water was quite gone from it, I saw a great bird which
look'd almost black picking up fish and busking in the
water, it looked like an Eagle and by its dimentions could
scarce be any other bird.

Thence I went into Scotland over the river Serke
[Sark] which is also flowed by the sea but in the summer
tyme is not soe deep, but can be pass'd over tho' pretty
deep but narrow; it affords good fish but all here about
which are called Borderers seem to be very poor people
which I impute to their sloth; Scotland this part of it is a

low marshy ground where they cutt turff and peate for
the fewell, tho' I should apprehend the sea might convey
coales to them; I see little that they are employ'd besides
fishing which makes provision plentiful, or else their
cutting and carving turff and peate which the women
and great girles bare legg'd does lead a horse which
draws a sort of carriage the wheeles like a dung-pott and
hold about 4 wheele barrows; these people tho' with
naked leggs are yet wrapp'd up in plodds a piece of
woollen like a blanket or else rideing hoods, and this
when they are in their houses; I tooke them for people
which were sick seeing 2 or 3 great wenches as tall and
bigg as any women sat hovering between their bed and
chimney corner all idle doing nothing, or at least was
not settled to any work, tho' it was nine of the clock
when I came thither, haveing gone 7 long miles that
morning.

This is a little Market town called Adison Bank, the
houses lookes just like the booths at a fair – I am sure I
have been in some of them that were tollerable dwellings
to these – they have no chimneys their smoke comes
out all over the house and there are great holes in the
sides of their houses which letts out the smoake when
they have been well smoaked in it; there is no roome in
their houses but is up to the thatch and in which are
2 or 3 beds even to their parlours and buttery; and
notwithstanding the cleaning of their parlour for me I
was not able to beare the roome; the smell of the hay
was a perfume and what I rather chose to stay and see
my horses eate their provender in the stable then to
stand in that roome, for I could not bring my self to sit

down; my Landlady offered me a good dish of fish and
brought me butter in a Lairdly Dish with the Clap bread,
but I could have no stomach to eate any of the food they
should order, and finding they had noe wheaten bread
I told her I could not eate their clapt oat bread, soe I
bought the fish she got for me which was full cheape
enough, nine pence for two pieces of Salmon halfe a one
neer a yard long and a very large Trout of an amber
coullour; soe drinking without eateing some of their
wine, which was exceeding good Clarret which they
stand conveniently for to have from France, and indeed
it was the best and truest French wine I have dranck this
seven year and very clear, I had the first tapping of the
little vessell and it was very fine.

Then I went up to their Church which looks rather
like some little house built of stone and bricke such as
our ordinary people in a village live in: the doores were
open and the seates and pulpit was in so disregarded a
manner that one would have thought there was no use
of it, but there is a parson which lives just by whose
house is the best in the place and they are all fine folks
in their Sundays cloathes; I observe the Church-yard is
full of grave stones pretty large with coates of armes and
some had a coronet on the eschutcheons cut in the stone;
I saw but one house that look'd like a house about a
quarter of a mile, which was some Gentlemans, that was
built 2 or 3 roomes and some over them of brick and
stone the rest were all like barns or hutts for cattle.

This is threescore miles from Edenborough and the
neerest town to this place is 18 miles, and there would not
have been much better entertainement or accomodation

and their miles are soe long in these countrys made me afraid to venture, least after a tedious journey I should not be able to get a bed I could lye in; it seemes there are very few towns except Edenburough Abberdeen and Kerk which can give better treatement to strangers, therefore for the most part persons that travell there go from one Noblemans house to another; those houses are all kind of Castles and they live great, tho' in so nasty a way, as all things are even in those houses, one has little stomach to eate or use any thing as I have been told by some that has travell'd there; and I am sure I mett with a sample of it enough to discourage my progress farther in Scotland; I attribute it wholly to their sloth for I see they sitt and do little – I think there were one or two at last did take spinning in hand at a lazy way; thence I tooke my fish to carry it to a place for the English to dress it, and repass'd the Serke and the River Essex and there I saw the common people, men women and children, take off their shooes and holding up their cloathes wade through the rivers when the tide was out; and truely some there were that when they come to the other side put on shoes and stockings and had fine plodds cast over them and their garb seemed above the common people, but this is their constant way of travelling from one place to another, if any river to pass they make no use of bridges and have not many.

I came to Long Town which is 3 long mile from Addison Bank and is called a Border and indeed is very like the Scots land; thence I cross'd over a tedious long heath to Brampton a mile over Lime river and here I had my dinner dress'd; thence to Mucks hall 6 miles;

here I pass'd by my Lord Carletons which stands in the midst of woods; you goe through lanes and little sort of woods or hedge rows and many little purling rivers or brooks out of the rocks.

At Muncks Hall I cross'd such another brooke and so out of Cumberland I entred Northumberland; this is the place the Judges dine its a sorry place for entertainment of such a company; here the Sherriffs meete them it being the entrance off Northumberland which is much like the other county; this it seemes Camden relates to be a Kingdom; this I am sure of the more I travell'd northward the longer I found the miles, I am sure these 6 miles and the other 6 miles to Hartwhistle might with modesty be esteemed double the number in most of the countys in England, especially in and about 30 or 40 miles off London; I did not go 2 of those miles in an hour; just at my entrance into Northumberland I ascended a very steep hill of which there are many, but one about 2 mile forward was exceeding steep full of great rocks and stone, some of it along on a row the remainder of the Picts walls or Fortification at the bottom of which was an old Castle the walls and towers of which was mostly standing; its a sort of black moorish ground and so wet I observ'd as my man rode up that sort of precipice or steep his horses heeles cast up water every step and their feete cut deepe in, even quite up to the top; such up and down hills and sort of boggy ground it was, and the night drawing fast on, the miles so long, that I tooke a Guide to direct me to avoid those ill places.

This Hartwhistle is a little town; there was one Inn but they had noe hay nor would get none, and when my

servants had got some else where they were angry and
would not entertaine me, so I was forced to take up in a
poor cottage which was open to the thatch and no
partitions but hurdles plaister'd; indeed the loft as they
called it which was over the other roome was shelter'd
but with a hurdle; here I was forced to take up my abode
and the Landlady brought me out her best sheetes which
serv'd to secure my own sheetes from her dirty blanckets,
and indeed I had her fine sheete with hook seams to
spread over the top of the clothes, but noe sleepe could
I get, they burning turff and their chimneys are sort of
flews or open tunnills that the smoake does annoy the
roomes.

This is but 12 miles from another part of Scotland, the
houses are but a little better built – its true the inside of
them are kept a little better; not far from this a mile or
two is a greate hill from which rises 3 rivers: the Teese
which is the border between Durham and York, the
Ouse that runns to Yorke and the river Tyne which
runns to Newcastle and is the divider of Northumberland
and Durham: this river Tyne runns 7 miles and then
joyns with the other river Tyne that comes out of Northumberland and so they run on to Newcastle; from
Hartwhistle I went pretty much up hill and down and
had the river Tyne much in view for 6 miles, then I
cross'd over it on a large stone bridge and so rode by its
bank or pretty much in sight of it on the other side to
Hexholme 6 mile more; this is one of the best towns in
Northumberland except Newcastle, which is one place
the sessions are kept for the shire, its built of stone and
looks very well, there are 2 gates to it many streetes

some are pretty broad all well pitch'd with a spacious Market place with a Town Hall on the Market Crosse; thence I went through the Lord Darentwaters parke just by his house which is an old building not very large; soe 3 mile in all to a little village where I cross'd over the Tyne on a long bridge of stone with many arches; the river is in some places broader than in others – its true at this tyme of the yeare being midsumer the springs are the lowest and the rivers shallow and where there is any rocks or stones left quite bare of water.

Thence I went 4 mile along by the Tyne, the road was good hard gravelly way for the most part but very steep up hills and down; on one of these I rode a pretty while with a great precipice on the right hand down to the river, it looked hazardous but the way was very broad; the river looked very reffreshing and the cattle coming to its sides and into it where shallow to coole themselves in the heate, for hitherto as I met with noe raines (notwithstanding the great raines that fell the 2 dayes before I left Woolsley and the little showers I had when I went to Holly Well I was not annoy'd with wet nor extream heate, the clouds being a shade to me by day and Gods good providence and protection allwayes; this after noon was the hottest day I met with but it was seasonable being in July.

As I drew nearer and nearer to Newcastle I met with and saw abundance of little carriages with a yoke of oxen and a pair of horses together, which is to convey the Coales from the pitts to the barges on the river; there is little sort of dung-potts I suppose they hold not above 2 or three chaudron; this is the Sea-coale which is pretty

much small coale though some is round coales, yet none
like the cleft coales; this is what the smiths use and it
cakes in the fire and makes a great heate, but it burns
not up light unless you put most round coales, which
will burn light, but then its soone gone and that part of
the coale never cakes; therefore the small sort is as good
as any, if its black and shineing that shews its goodness;
this country all about is full of this Coale the sulpher of
it taints the aire and it smells strongly to strangers; upon
a high hill 2 mile from Newcastle I could see all about
the country which was full of coale pitts.

Newcastle lies in a bottom very low it appears from
this hill and a greate flatt I saw all by the river Tyne
which runns along to Tinmouth 5 or 6 miles off which
could see very plaine and the Scheld [North Shields]
which is the key or fort at the mouth of the river which
disembogues it self into the sea; all this was in view on
this high hill, which I descended 5 mile more in all nine
from that place.

Newcastle is a town and county of it self standing part in Northumberland part in the Bishoprick of
Durham, the river Tyne being the division; its a noble
town tho' in a bottom, it most resembles London of any
place in England, its buildings lofty and large of brick
mostly or stone; the streetes are very broad and handsome and very well pitch'd and many of them with very
fine Cunduits of water in each, allwayes running into a
large stone Cistern for every bodyes use, there is one
great streete where in the Market Crosse there was one
great Cunduit with two spouts which falls into a large
Fountaine paved with stone which held at least 2 or 3

hodsheads for the inhabitants; there are 4 gates which
are all double gates with a sort of bridge between each;
the West gate which I entred I came by a large building
of bricke within brick walls which is the hall for the
asizes and session for the shire of Northumberland; this
is Newcastle on the Tyne and is a town and county;
there is a noble building in the middle of the town all of
stone for an Exchange on stone pillars severall rows; on
the top is a building of a very large Hall for the judges
to keep the assizes for the town, there is another roome
for the Major and Councill, and another for the jury, out
of the large roome which is the hall, and opens into a
balcony which lookes out on the river and the key; its a
lofty good building of stone, very uniforme on all sides
with stone pillars in the fronts both to the streete and
market place and to the waterside; there is a fine clock
on the top just as the Royal Exchange has; the key is a
very fine place and looks it self like an exchange being
very broad and soe full of merchants walking to-an-
againe, and it runs off a great length with a great many
steps down to the water for the conveniency of landing
or boateing their goods, and is full of cellars or ware
houses; the harbour is full of shipps but none that is
above 2 or 300 tun can come up quite to the key, its
a town of greate trade.

There is one large Church built of stone with a very
high tower finely carv'd full of spires and severall devices
in the carving all stone; the Quire is neate as is the whole
Church and curious carving in wood on each side the
Quire, and over the font is a greate piramidy of wood
finely carv'd full of spires; there was a Castle in this town

but now there is noe remaines of it but some of the walls
which are built up in houses, and soe only appears as a
great hill or ascent which in some places is 30 or 40 steps
advance to the streetes that are built on the higher
ground where the Castle was; there was one place soe
like Snow Hill in London with a fine Conduite; their
shops are good and are of distinct trades, not selling
many things in one shop as is the custom in most country
towns and cittys; here is one market for Corne another
for Hay besides all other things which takes up two or
three streetes; Satturday was their biggest Market day
which was the day I was there and by reason of the
extreame heate resolved to stay till the sun was low ere
I proceeded farther, so had the opportunity of seeing
most of the Market which is like a faire for all sorts of
provision and goods and very cheape: I saw one buy a
quarter of lamb for 8 pence and 2 pence a piece good
large poultry; here is leather, woollen and linnen and all
sorts of stands for baubles; they have a very indifferent
sort of cheese, little things looks black on the outside
and soft sower things.

There is a very pleasant bowling-green a little walke
out of the town with a large gravel walke round it with
two rows of trees on each side makeing it very shady;
there is a fine entertaineing house that makes up the
fourth side before which is a paved walke under pyasoes
[piazzas] of bricke; there is a pretty garden by the side
shady walk, its a sort of Spring Garden where the Gentlemen and Ladyes walke in the evening; there is a green
house in the garden; its a pleasant walke to the town by
the walls; there is one broad walke by the side of the

town runns a good length made with coale ashes and so well trodden and the raines makes it firm; there is a walke all round the walls of the town, there is a good free Schoole, 5 Churches.

I went to see the Barber Surgeons Hall which was within a pretty garden walled in, full of flowers and greenes in potts and in the borders; its a good neat building of brick, there I saw the roome with a round table in it, railed round with seates or benches for the conveniency in their disecting and anatomiseing a body and reading lectures on all parts; there was two bodyes that had been anatomised, one the bones were fastned with wires the other had had the flesh boyled off and some of the ligeaments remained and dryed with it, and so the parts were held together by its own muscles and sinews that were dryed with it; over this was another roome in which was the skin of a man that was taken off after he was dead and dressed and so was stuff'd the body and limbs, it look'd and felt like a sort of parchment; in this roome I could take a view of the whole town, it standing on high ground and a pretty lofty building.

Just by is a very good Hospital for 14 widdows off tradesmen of the town, 2 good roomes a piece; a walke under a pyasoe with pillars of brickwork as is the whole building; there is a large Fountaine or Cunduite of water for their use and an open green before their house all walled in, its in the Major and Aldermens disposition, there is 2 or 300 pound a yeare to it I thinke its 10 pound apiece; there is a very good fountaine belongs to it and there is a fine Bridge over the Tyne river with 9 arches all built on as London Bridge is, which enters you into

Durham, and on this side of the bridge are so many streetes and buildings just like Southwarke; its a little town but all is in the liberty of the County town of Newcastle and soe called, but its all in the Diocess of Durham; through part of this you do ascend a greate height and steepness which is full of rocky stony stepps and afterwards the hill continues when out of the town till it has set you as high as on the former hill on the other side the town, which I entred out of Northumberland, and as that gave a large prospect of the town and whole country aboute on that side, soe this gives as pleasing a sight of it on this side, and the whole river and shipps in the harbour.

Through Worcester, Gloucester, Bristol to Wells and Taunton

From Woosly to Haywood Parke 2 mile and home againe 2 mile; from Woolsley to Kank town [Cannock] 6 mile thence to Woolverhampton 6 mile; I went more in sight of Sir Walter Rochly [Wrottesley] which stands very finely on a hill and woods by it lookes very stately, these miles are very long thro' lanes; I passed by a fine house Prestwitch [Prestwood], Mr Philip Folies a pretty seate; in a parke a mile beyond there is another house of the same Gentlemans; here we had the inconveniency of meeting the Sheriffs of Staffordshire just going to provide for the reception of the Judges and Officers of the Assizes, whose coaches and Retinue meeteing our Company which was encreased with Cosen Fiennes's coach and horsemen which made us difficult to pass each other in the hollow wayes and lanes; thence to the Seven Starres where we baited; thence 2 miles farther we entred out of Staffordshire into Worcestershire, to Broad water a place where are severall fullers and dyers mills; thence on the right hand are forging mills for iron works which belong to Mr Thomas Folie; there is a rocky hill in which is a Roome cut out in the rocks.

On the left hand you goe 7 mile to Ambusly [Ombersley] a very sad heavy way all sand, you goe just at Kederminster town end, which is a large town much employ'd about the worstead trade spinning and weaving; we also rode by Sir John Packingtons house on the left hand on the hill just by Droitwitch, where are the 3 salt springs divided by a fresh spring that runs by it; of this salt water they boyle much salt that turns to good account.

All the way from the Seven Starrs where we baited to Ambusly the road was full of the Electers of the Parliament men coming from the choice of the Knights of the Shire, which spake as they were affected, some for one some for another, and some were larger in their judgments than others, telling their reason much according to the good liquors operation and of these people all the publick houses were filled that it was a hard matter to get Lodging or Entertainment; we entered Worcester town next day just as the cerimony of the Election was performing and soe they declared it in favour of Mr Welsh and Sir John Packington.

Four miles more to this town – from Broad water in all is 11 mile – Worcester town which is washed by the river Severn; its a large Citty, 12 Churches, the streetes most of them broad, the buildings some of them are very good and lofty; its encompass'd with a wall which has 4 gates that are very strong; the Market place is large; there is a Guildhall besides the Market house which stands on pillars of stone; the Cathedrall stands in a large yard pitch'd, its a lofty magnificent building the Quire has good wood carv'd and a pretty organ; there is one tombstone stands in the middle of the Quire by the railes on which lyes the Effigies of King John; the left side of the alter is Prince Arthurs tomb of plaine marble in a fine Chappell which is made all of stone finely carv'd both the inside and the outside is very curiously carv'd in all sorts of works and arms, beasts and flowers; under it lyes the statues of severall Bishops, beyond this are two tombstones with the figure of the body in their proper dress of 2 Saxon Bishops on the pavement; the painting of the windows are good and they are pretty large and lofty tho' nothing comparable to the Cathedrall at York; the tower is high and about the middle of it you may walk round the inside and look down into the body of the Church just as it is in York; just against the pulpit in the body of the Church is a little organ to set the Psalme, the font is all of white marble and a carv'd cover of wood.

From Worcester we pass'd a large stone bridge over the Severn on which were many Barges that were tow'd up by the strength of men 6 or 8 at a tyme; the water just by the town encompasses a little piece of ground full of willows and so makes it an island, part of which turns Mills; thence I went 4 mile where I cross the River Thames on a stone bridge; this runs to Whitborne, and is a very rapid streame especially after raines, which just before we begun our Journey had fallen, and made the roads which are all lanes full of stones and up hills and down soe steep that with the raines the waters stood or else ran down the hills, which made it exceeding bad for travelling; when we had gone 7 mile at a little Parish you enter out of Worcester into Herriffordshire and soe 7 mile farther to Stretton Grandsom and New House my Cos'n Fiennes's; this is the worst way I ever went in Worcester or Herrifordshire – its allways a deep sand

and soe in the winter and with muck is bad way, but this
being in August it was strange and being so stony made
it more difficult to travell.

From thence I went to Stoake 4 miles, where I saw
Mr Folies new house which was building and will be
very fine when compleated; there is to be 3 flat fronts to
the gardens sides, the right wing of the house is the
severall appartments for the family, 2 drawing roomes
and bed chambers and closets opening both on a terrass
of free stone pavements each end, and the middle there
is stone stepps goes down on each side with half paces
to the garden, which is by more stepps descending one
below another; the other wing is to the other garden
and are to be roomes of state which lookes towards
Herrifford town: this is to be coupled together with a
large hall which composes the front and is of stone work,
the rest is brick only coyn'd with stone and the windows
stone, and is in forme of a halfe moone each side with
arches to the severall offices and stables; to this front
which is to be the entrance large opening iron spike gates
which lookes into their Grounds and Meddowes below
it of a great length with rows of trees to the river; the
roofe is cover'd with slatt which shines and very much
represents lead, its adorn'd round the edges with stone
figures and flower potts; there is a noble Parck and
woods behind; it will be very fine when finished, now
I saw it only in the outside shell and plattform.

Thence I returned to Newhouse 4 mile; then I went
to Canaan Froom a mile, and one mile back which was
2 mile more; then to Stretton four tymes and back which
was 8 mile; then from New house to Aldbery [Alders

End] 5 mile, thence to Marlow [Marcle] 3 mile and there entred Gloucestershire; they are pretty long miles and in the winter deep way though now it was pretty good travelling; its 8 mile beyond to Glocester town (tho' in most places near London this would be reckon'd 20 miles) you may see the town 4 miles off.

Glocester town lyes all along on the bancks of the Severn and soe look'd like a very huge place being stretch'd out in length, its a low moist place therefore one must travel on Causseys which are here in good repair; I pass'd over a bridge where two armes of the river meetes where the tyde is very high and rowles in the sand in many places and causes those Whirles or Hurricanes that will come on storms with great impetuosity; thence I proceeded over another bridge into the town whose streetes are very well pitch'd large and cleane; there is a faire Market place and Hall for the assizes which happened just as we came there, soe had the worst Entertainment and noe accomodation but in a private house – things ought not to be deare here but Strangers are allwayes imposed on and at such a publick tyme alsoe they make their advantages – here is a very large good Key on the river; they are supply'd with coales by the shipps and barges which makes it plentifull, they carry it on sledgs thro' the town, its the great Warwickshire coale I saw unloading; here they follow knitting, stockings gloves wastcoates and peticoates and sleeves all of cotten, and others spinn the cottens.

The Cathedrall or Minster is large lofty and very neate, the Quire pretty; at the entrance there is a seate over head for the Bishop to sit in to hear the sermon preached in the body of the Church, and therefore the organs in the Quire was on one side which used to be at the entrance; there was a tomb stone in the middle with a statue of Duke Roberts second son to William the Conquerours son, with his legs across, as is the manner of all those that went to the holy warre – this is painted and resembles marble tho' it is but wood and soe light as by one finger you may move it up, there is an iron grate over it; at the alter the painting is soe fine that the tapistry and pillars and figure of Moses and Aaron soe much to the life you would at least think it Carv'd; there are 12 Chappells all stone finely carv'd on the walls and rooffs, the windows are pretty large and high with very good paintings, there is a large window just over the alter, but between it and the alter is a hollow walled in, on each side, which is a Whispering place; speake never so low just in the wall at one end the person at the other end shall heare it plaine, tho' those which stand by you shall not heare you speake, its the wall carrys the voyce – this seems not quite soe wonderfull as I have heard for the large roome in Mountague House (soe remarkable for fine painting) I have been in it and when the doores are shutt its so well suited in the walls you cannot tell where to find the doore if a stranger, and its a large roome every way; I saw a Lady stand at one corner and turn her self to the wall and whisper'd, the voice came very cleer and plaine to the Company that stood at the crosse corner of the roome soe that it could not be carry'd by the side wall, it must be the arch overhead which was a great height.

But to return to the Church: the tower was 203 stepps,

the large bell I stood upright in but it was not so bigg as the great Tom of Lincoln, this bell at Glocester is raised by ten and rung by 6 men; on the tower leads you have a prospect of the whole town, gardens and buildings and grounds beyond, and the river Severn in its twistings and windings; here are the fine Lamprys taken in great quantetys in their season of which they make pyes and potts and convey them to London or else where, such a present being fitt for a king; this and the Charr fish are equally rare and valuable; here are very good Cloysters finely adorn'd with fretwork, here is the Colledge and Library but not stored with many books; I think this was all the remarkables in Glocester.

From thence I went in Company all this while with my Cos'n Filmer and family; we came to Nymphsffield after haueing ascended a very steep narrow and stony hill 10 mile to Nympsfield, all bad way, but the 20 mile afterwards made up for its badness for these were exceeding good wayes: 2 mile to Cold harbour thence 15 to Landsdon: long but bowling green way; here I passed by Babington the Duke of Beauffort's house, stands in a Parke on an advanc'd ground with rows of trees on all sides which runns a good length and you may stand on the leads and look 12 wayes down to the parishes and grounds beyond all thro' glides or visto of trees; the Gardens are very fine and Water works.

On Landsdon Summersetshire begins, which is a very pleasant hill for to ride on for aire and prospect; I went 3 mile over it which leads to the Bath down a vast steep descent of a stony narrow way, as is all the wayes down into the town; the Bath is a pretty place full of good

houses all for the accomodation of the Company that
resort thither to drink or bathe in the summer; the
streetes are faire and well pitch'd, they carry most things
on sledges and the company use all the morning the
Chaires of Bayes [baize] to carry them to the Bath, soe
they have the Chaire or Sedan to carry them in visits;
there is a very fine Hall which is set on stone pillars
which they use for the balls and dancing, this is the only
new thing since I was at the Bath before except the fine
adornements on the Cross in the Cross Bath, fine carving
of stone with the English arms and saints and cupids
according to the phancye and religion of King James the
Seconds Queen Mary of Modina, as part of her thanks
and acknowledgments to the Saints or Virgin Mary for
the Welsh Prince she imposed on us; and from the Bath
I went westward to Bristol over Landsdown 10 mile and
passed thro' Kingswood, and was met with a great many
horses passing and returning loaden with coals dug just
thereabout; they give 12 pence a horse load which carryes
two bushells, it makes very good fires, this is the cakeing
coale.

Bristol lyes low in a bottom the greatest part of the
town, tho' one end of it you have a pretty rise of ground;
there are 19 Parish Churches beside the Cathedrall which
has nothing fine or curious in it; the buildings of the
town are pretty high most of timber work, the streetes
are narrow and something darkish, because the roomes
on the upper storys are more jutting out, soe contracts
the streete and the light; the suburbs are better buildings
and more spacious streetes; there are at one place as you
enter the town 2 almshouses 6 men and 6 women apiece

at each, there is alsoe at another part of the town a noble almshouse more like a gentlemans house that is all of stone work, a handsome court with gates and pallisadoes before four grass plotts divided by paved walks and a walk round the same; the one side is for the women the other for the men, the middle building is 2 kitchins for either and a middle roome in common for washing and brewing, over all is a Chappell; they have gardens behind it with all things convenient, they have their coales and 3 shillings per weeke allowed to each to maintaine them; this is for decayed tradesmen and wives that have lived well, its set up and allowed to by Mr Coleson a merchant in London.

This town is a very great tradeing citty as most in England, and is esteemed the largest next London; the river Aven, that is flowed up by the sea into the Severn and soe up the Aven to the town, beares shipps and barges up to the key, where I saw the harbour was full of shipps carrying coales and all sorts of commodityes to other parts; the Bridge is built over with houses just as London Bridge is, but its not so bigg or long, there are 4 large arches here; they have little boates which are called Wherryes such as we use on the Thames, soe they use them here to convey persons from place to place; and in many places there are signes to many houses that are not Publick houses just as it is in London; the streetes are well pitch'd and preserved by their useing sleds to carry all things about.

There is a very faire Market place and an Exchange set on stone pillars; in another place there is a very high and magnificent Cross built all of the stone or sort of marble of the country, its in the manner of Coventry Cross, a piramedy form running up of a great height with severall divisions in niches where is King Johns Effigy and severall other Kings round and adorned with armes and figures of beasts and birds and flowers, great part of it gilt and painted, and soe terminates in a spire on the top; the lower part is white like marble; just by the water side is a long rope yard which is encompass'd with trees on either side which are lofty and shady, therefore its made choice of for the Company of the town to take the diversion of walking in the evening; this compasses round a large space of ground which is called the Marsh, a green ground; there was noe remaines of the Castle; there are 12 gates to the Citty, there is a very large conduit by the key finely carv'd all stone, this conveys the water about the town but all the water has a brackish taste.

There is one Church which is an entire worke all of stone, noe timbers but the rafters and beames belonging to the roofe and the seates they sit in, the leads are very high and large and very neate kept, the tower 150 stepps up, on which the whole Citty is discover'd which by reason of the good gardens and grounds within its walls is a very large tract of ground in the whole; there you see the Colledge Green in which stands the Cathedrall and the Doctors houses which are not very fine built of stone; there are some few monuments in this Church with good carvings of stone round the tombs and some Effigies; there are 8 bells in this Church, there is 2 men goes to the ringing the biggest bell.

From thence I went 2 miles to the hott spring of water

which lookes exceeding cleer and is as warm as new milk and much of that sweetness; this is just by St Vincents Rocks that are great clifts which seeme as bounds to the river Aven this channell was hewn out of those rocks they digg the Bristol Diamonds which look very bright and sparkling and in their native rudeness have a great lustre and are pointed and like the diamond cutting; I had a piece just as it came out of the rock with the rock on the back side, and it appeared to me as a cluster of diamonds polish'd and irregularly cut; some of these are hard and will endure the cutting and pollishing by art and soe they make rings and earings of them; the harder the stone is the more valuable, which differences the true diamond, that will bear the fire or the greatest force, and cannot be divided nor cut but by some of it self diamond dust, being the only way they can cut diamonds that it self is capable of impressing carracters on glass; here I ferry'd over the Avon that comes up to the town with a great tyde in two parts; about 6 mile off it joyns the Severn which now begins to swell into a vast river of 7 mile over, before it enters the sea.

Then I went to Aston a mile from the water side thro' a fine park, an old large house, and thence I passed over large downs and saw 2 other good houses built of stone with towers on the top and severall rows of trees leading to them which made them appear very fine; soe to Oakey Hole [Wookey Hole] which from the water side where I ferry'd is esteemed but 15 long mile (its the same distance from Bristole but I would not goe back to the town, but twere better I had for I made it at least 17 mile that way).

Oacky Hole is a large cavity under ground like Poole

Hole in Darbyshire only this seemes to be a great hill above it; its full of great rocks and stones lying in it just as if they were hewen out of a quarry and laid down all in the ground; the wall and roofe is all a rocky stone, there is a lofty space they call the Hall and another the Parlour and another the Kitchen; the entrance of each one out of another is with greate stooping under rocks that hang down almost to touch the ground; beyond this is a Cistern allwayes full of water, it looks cleer to the bottom which is all full of stones as is the sides, just like candy or like the branches they put in the boyling of copperace for the copperice to crust about it, this in the same manner so that the water congeales here into stone and does as it were bud or grow out one stone out of another; where ever this water drops it does not weare the rock in hollow as some other such subterranian caves does, but it hardens and does encrease the stone and that in a roundness as if it candy'd as it fell, which I am of opinion it does, so it makes the rocks grow and meete each other in some places.

They fancy many Resemblances in the rocks, as in one place an organ, and in another 2 little babys, and in another part a head which they call the Porters head, and another a shape like a dog; they phancy one of the rocks resembles a woman with a great belly which the country people call the Witch which made this cavity under ground for her enchantments; the rocks are glistering and shine like diamonds, and some you climbe over where one meetes with the congealed drops of water just like iceicles hanging down; some of the stone is white like alabaster and glisters like mettle; you walke for the most part in the large spaces called the Roomes on a sandy floore the roofe so lofty one can scarce discern the top and carry's a great eccho, soe that takeing up a great stone as much as a man can heave up to his head and letting it fall gives a report like a Cannon, which they frequently trye and call the Shooteing the Cannons; at the farther end you come to a water call'd the Well, its of a greate depth and compass tho' by the light of the candles you may discern the rock encompassing it as a wall round; these hollows are generally very cold and damp by reason of the waters distilling continually, which is very cold as ice almost when I put my hand into the Cistern.

These roads are full of hills and those, some of them, high ridge of hills, which does discover a vast prospect all wayes; behind me I saw a great valley full of inclosures and lessar hills by which you ascend these heights which are all very fruitfull and woody; also I could see the Severn when encreased to its breadth of 7 mile over, and there it disembogues into the sea; then it gave me a prospect forward of as large a vale replenish'd with fruitefull hills and trees and good ground; thence I could discern Glassenbury tower, this was Maiden Hill, just beyond the little town of same name, and soe by degrees descending from a higher to a lower hill, which had its ascents as well as its descents, which makes the miles seem and are indeed long tracts of ground.

From Ocley Hole I went to Wells which was on an even ground one mile farther; this Wells is what must be reckoned halfe a Citty, this and the Bath makeing up but one Bishops See; here are two Churches with the

Cathedrall; the Cathedral has the greatest curiosity for carv'd work in stone, the West Front is full of all sorts of figures, the 12 apostles, the King and Queen with angells and figures of all forms as thick one to another as can be, and soe almost all round the Church; the assizes was in the town which filled it like a faire, and little stands for selling things was in all the streetes; there I saw the Town Hall – the streetes are well pitch'd – and a large market place and shambles; the Bishops Pallace is in a park moated round, nothing worth notice in it; St Andrews Well which gives name to the town bubbles up so quick a spring and becomes the head of two little rivers which encreases a little way of[f] into good rivers.

Thence I went to Glassenbury, 4 miles a pretty levell way till just you come to the town; then I ascended a stony hill and went just by the tower which is on a green round riseing ground, there is only a little tower remaines like a Beacon; it had Bells formerly in it, and some superstition observ'd there but now its broken down on one side; from this I descended a very steep stony way into the town; Glassenbury tho' in ancient tymes was a renowned place where was founded the first monastery, its now a ragged poor place and the Abbey has only the Kitchen remaining in it, which is a distinct building round like a pigeon house all stone; the walls of the Abby here and there appeares, and some little places and the cellar or vault which if they cast a stone into the place it gives a great echo, and the country people sayes its the Devil set there on a tun of money, which makes that noise least they should take it away from him; there is the Holly Thorn growing on a chimney; this the superstitious covet much and have gott some of it for their gardens and soe have almost quite spoiled it, which did grow quite round a chimney tunnell in the stone; here is a very pretty Church, a good tower well carv'd all stone 160 stepps up; walking in the tower I could have a prospect of the whole place which appeared very ragged and decayed; the Church is neate, there is the Effigie of the Abbot on a tombstone carved all about with Eschuteons of a Camell, and round it an inscription or motto in old Latin and an old Caracter; it was phancy of his Stewards who was a very faithfull dilligent servant, and as he made use of those creatures in his masters service that were strong and industrious, so the motto described his services under that resemblance; the Effigee was very curious and with rings on the fingers, but in Monmouths tyme the soldiers defaced it much.

From thence to Taunton 16 long miles through many small places and scattering houses, through lanes full of stones and, by the great raines just before, full of wet and dirt, I passed over a large common or bottom of deep black land which is bad for the rider but good for the abider, as the proverb is; this was 2 or 3 mile long and pass'd and repass'd a river as it twin'd about at least ten tymes over stone bridges; this river comes from Bridgewater 7 mile, the tyde comes up beyond Bridge-water even within 3 mile of Taunton, its flowed by the tyde which brings up the barges with coale to this place, after having pass'd a large common which on either hand leads a great waye good rich land with ditches and willow trees all for feeding cattle, and here at this little place where the boates unlade the coale the packhorses comes, and takes it in sacks and so carryes it to the places all about; this is the Sea coale brought from Bristole, the horses carry 2 bushell at a tyme which at the place cost 18d. and when its brought to Taunton cost 2 shillings; the roads were full of these carryers going and returning.

Taunton is a large town haveing houses of all sorts of buildings both brick and stone but mostly timber and plaister; its a very neate place and looks substantial as a place of good trade; you meete all sorts of country women wrapp'd up in the manteles called West Country rockets, a large mantle doubled together of a sort of serge, some are linsywolsey, and a deep fringe or fag at the lower end; these hang down some to their feete some only just below the wast, in the summer they are all in white garments of this sort, in the winter they are in red ones; I call them garments because they never go out without them and this is the universal fashion in Sommerset and Devonshire and Cornwall; here is a good Market Cross well carv'd and a large Market House on pillars for the corn; I was in the largest Church, it was mending, it was pretty large, the alter stood table ways in the middle of the Chancell; there was one good stone statue stood in the wall the Effigie was very tall in a ruff and long black dress like some Religious with his gloves and book in his hand; there were severall little monuments with inscriptions round them; they have encompass'd the Church-yard with a new brick wall and handsom iron gates; there is a large space called the Castle yard and some remaines of the Castle walls and buildings, which is fitted up for a good dwelling house.

Through Devonshire to Land's End

From thence I went to Wellington (they call it but 5 mile but its a long 7 tho' the way was pretty good) this is a Little Market town: thence to Culimton 11 mile more, but indeed these were very long miles; the hostler at Tanton did say, tho' they were reckon'd but 16 miles it really was a good 20 miles, and I am much of that mind; I mostly pass'd through lanes, I entred into Devonshire 5 mile off from Wellington just on a high Ridge of hills which discovers a vast prospect on each side full of inclosures and lesser hills, which is the description of most part of the West; you could see large tracts of grounds full of enclosures, good grass and corn beset with quicksetts and hedge rows, and these lesser hills, which are scarce perceivable on the ridge of the uppermost yet the least of them have a steep ascent and descent to pass them.

Culimton is a good little Market town, a Market Cross and another set on stone pillars (such a one was at Wellington but on brick work pillars); here was a large Meeteing of neer 4 or 500 people, they have a very good Minister but a young man, I was glad to see soe many tho' they were but of the meaner sort, for indeed its the poor receive the Gospell, and there are in most of the market towns in the West very good Meeteings; this little place was one continued long streete, but few houses that struck out of the streete.

From thence 10 mile to Exetter up hills and down as before till one attaines those uppermost ridges of all which discovers the whole valley, then you sometymes goe a mile or two on a Down till the brow of the hill begins in a descent on the other side; this Citty appears to view 2 mile distant from one of those heights, and also the River Ex which runs to Topshum where the shipps comes up to the barre; this is 7 mile by water, from which they are attempting to make navigeable to the town which will be of mighty advantage to have shipps come up close to the town to take in their serges, which now they are forced to send to Topshum on horses by land which is about 4 mile by land; they had just agreed with a man that was to accomplish this work for which they were to give 5 or 6000£, who had made a beginning on it.

Exeter is a town very well built the streets are well pitch'd spacious noble streetes and a vast trade is carryd on; as Norwitch is for coapes callamanco and damaske soe this is for Serges – there is an increadible quantety of them made and sold in the town; their market day is Fryday which supplys with all things like a faire almost; the markets for meate fowle fish garden things and the dairy produce takes up 3 whole streetes, besides the large Market house set on stone pillars which runs a great length on which they lay their packs of serges, just by it is another walke within pillars which is for the yarne; the whole town and country is employ'd for at least 20 mile round in spinning, weaveing, dressing, and scouring, fulling and drying of the serges, it turns the most money in a weeke of anything in England, one weeke with another there is 10000 pound paid in ready money, sometymes 15000 pound; the weavers brings in their serges and must have their money which they employ to provide them yarne to goe to work againe; there is alsoe a Square Court with penthouses round where the Malters are with mault, oat meal, but the serge is the chief manufacture; there is a prodigious quantety of their serges they never bring into the market but are in hired roomes which are noted for it, for it would be impossible to have it altogether.

The carryers I met going with it as thick all entring into town, with their loaded horses, they bring them all just from the loome and soe they are put into the fulling-mills, but first they will clean and scour their roomes with them – which by the way gives noe pleasing perfume to a roome, the oyle and grease, and I should think it would rather foull a roome than cleanse it because of the oyle but I perceive its otherwise esteemed by them, which will send to their acquaintances that are tuckers the dayes the serges comes in for a rowle to clean their house, this I was an eye witness of; then they lay them in soack in vrine [urine] then they soape them and soe put them into the fulling-mills and soe worke them in the mills drye till they are thick enough, then they turne water into them and so scower them; the mill does draw out and gather in the serges, its a pretty divertion to see it, a sort of huge notch'd timbers like great teeth, one would thinke it should injure the serges but it does not, the mills draws in with such a great violence that if one stands neere it, and it catch a bitt of your garments it would be ready to draw in the person even in a trice; when they are thus scour'd they drye them in racks strained out, which are as thick set one by another as will permitt the dresser to pass between, and huge large fields occupy'd this way almost all round the town which is to the river side; then when drye they burle them picking out all knotts, then fold them with a paper between every fold and so sett them on an iron plaite and screw down the press on them, which has another iron plaite on the top under which is a furnace of fire of coales, this is the hott press; then they fold them exceeding exact and then press them in a cold press; some they dye but the most are sent up for London white.

I saw the severall fatts [vats] they were a dying in, of black, yellow, blew, and green – which two last coullours are dipp'd in the same fatt, that which makes it differ is what they were dipp'd in before, which makes them either green or blew; they hang the serges on a great beame or great pole on the top of the fatt and so keep turning it from one to another, as one turns it off into the fatt the other rowles it out of it, soe they do it backwards and forwards till its tinged deep enough of the coullour; their furnace that keepes their dye panns boyling is all under that roome, made of coale fires; there was in a roome by it self a fatt for the scarlet, that being a very chargeable dye noe waste must be allow'd in that; indeed I think they make as fine a coullour as their Bow dies [dyes] are in London; these rolers I spake off; two men does continually role on and off the pieces of serges till dipp'd enough, the length of these pieces are or should hold out 26 yards.

This Citty does exceedingly resemble London for, besides these buildings I mention'd for the severall Markets, there is an Exchange full of shops like our Exchanges are, only its but one walke along as was the Exchange at Salisbury House in the Strand; there is also a very large space railed in just by the Cathedrall, with walks round it, which is called the Exchange for Merchants, that constantly meete twice a day just as they do in London; there are 17 Churches in the Citty and 4 in the subburbs; there is some remaines of the Castle walls, they make use of the rooms within side for the assizes; there is the two barrs besides, being large rooms with seates and places convenient, and jury roome; here is a large walke at the entrance between rowes of pillars; there is besides this just at the market place a Guild Hall the entrance of which is a large place set on stone pillars, beyond which are the roomes for the session or any town affaires to be adjusted; behind this building there is a vast Cistern which holds upwards of 600 hodsheads of water which supplyes by pipes the whole Citty, this Cistern is replenish'd from the river which is on purpose turned into a little channell by it self to turn the mill and fills the Engine that casts the water into the truncks which convey it to this Cistern; the Water Engine is like those at Islington at Darby as I have seen, and is what now they make use of in diverse places either to supply them with water or to draine a marsh or overplus of water.

The river X [Exe] is a fine streame; they have made severall bays or wires above the bridge which casts the water into many channells for the conveniencys of turning all their mills, by which meanes they have composed a little island, for at the end it againe returns into its own united channell; those wires makes great falls into the water it comes with great violence, here they catch the salmon as they leap, with speares; the first of these bayes is a very great one; there is one below the bridge which must be taken away when the navigation is compleate, for they will need all their water together to fill it to a depth to carry the shipps, for just by the bridge is the key design'd, or that which now is already they will enlarge to that place; just by this key is the Custome house, an open space below with rows of pillars which they lay in goods just as its unladen out of the shipps in case of wet, just by are severall little roomes for Land-waiters, etc., then you ascend up a handsome pair of staires into a large roome full of desks and little partitions for the writers and accountants, its was full of books and files of paper, by it are two other roomes which are used in the same way when there is a greate deale of bussiness; there are severall good Conduites to supply the Citty with water besides that Cistern, there is alsoe a very fine Market Cross.

The Cathedral at Exettor is preserv'd in its outside adornments beyond most I have seen, there remaining more of the fine carv'd worke in stone the figures and nitches full and in proportion, tho' indeed I cannot say it has that great curiosity of work and variety as the great Church at Wells; its a lofty building in the inside the largest pair of organs I have ever seen with fine carving of wood which runs up a great height and made a magnificent appearance; the Quire is very neate but the Bishops seate or throne was exceeding, and very high, and the carving very fine, and took up a great compass, full of all variety of figures, something like the worke over the Arch-Bishops throne in St Pauls London, but this was larger if not so curious; there was severall good Monuments and Effigies of Bishops, there was one of a Judge and his Lady that was very curious their garments embroyder'd all marble and gilt and painted; there was a very large good Library in which was a press that had an anatomy of a woman; the tower is 167 steps up on which I had a view of the whole town which is generally well built; I saw the Bishops Pallace and Garden; there is a long walke as well as broad enclosed with rows of lofty trees which made it shady and very pleasant, which went along by the ditch and banck on which the town wall stands; there are 5 gates to the town; there is alsoe another long walke within shady trees on the other side of the town, which leads to the grounds where the drying frames are set up for the serges.

From thence I pass'd the bridge across the River Ex to Chedly [Chudleigh], which was 9 mile, mostly lanes and a continual going up hill and down, some of them pretty steep hills, and all these lesser hills as I have observ'd rises higher and higher till it advances you upon the high ridge, which discovers to view the great valleys below full of those lesser hills and inclosures, with quick-sett hedges and trees, and rich land; but the roads are not to be seen, being all along in lanes cover'd over with the shelter of the hedges and trees; then when I was on the top hill I went 3 or 4 miles on an open down which brought me to the edge of another such a ridge, which was by some steps to be descended, as it was gained, by the lesser hills one below another till I came to the bottom; and then I had about 2 or 3 mile along on a plaine or common, which for the most part are a little moorish by reason of their receiving the water that draines from the severall great hills on either side, and so then I am to rise up another such a range of hills, and as neer as I could compute in my rideing it was 6 or 7 mile between one high ridge of hills to that over against it, whereas were there a bridge over from one top to the other it could not be 2 mile distant; but this does give them the advantage of severall acres of land by reason of the many hills, which if drawn out on plaines as in some other parts would appear much vaster tracts of land; on these hills as I said one can discern little besides inclosures hedges and trees, rarely can see houses unless you are just descending to them, they allwayes are placed in holes as it were, and you have a precipice to go down to come at them; the lanes are full of stones and dirt for the most part, because they are so close the sun and wind cannot come at them, soe that in many places you travell on Causeys which are uneven also for want of a continued repaire.

From Chedly to Ashburton is 11 mile more, in all 20 mile from Exeter, the roads being much the same as before; this Ashburton is a poor little town, bad was the best Inn; its a Market town and here are a great many Descenters and those of the most considerable persons in the town, there was a Presbiterian an Anabaptist and Quakers meeting.

Thence I went for Plymouth 24 long miles, and here the roades contracts and the lanes are exceeding narrow and so cover'd up you can see little about, an army might be marching undiscover'd by any body, for when you are on those heights that shews a vast country about, you cannot see one road; the wayes now became so difficult that one could scarcely pass by each other, even the single horses, and so dirty in many places and just a track for one horses feete, and the banks on either side so neer, and were they not well secured and mended with stones struck close like a drye wall every where when they discover the bancks to breake and molder down which else would be in danger of swallowing up the way quite, for on these bancks which are some of them naturall rocks and quarrys others mended with such stone or slate struck edgewayes to secure them, for the quicksetts and trees that grow on these bancks loosen the mold and so makes it molder downe sometymes.

I pass'd through severall little places and over some stone bridges; the waters are pretty broad soe these are 4 or 5 arches most bridges, all stone; the running of the waters is with a huge rushing by reason of the stones which lye in the water, some of them great rocks which gives some interruption to the current which finding another way either by its sides or mounting over part of it causes the frothing of the water and the noise, the rivers being full of stones bigger or less.

About 4 or 5 mile from Ashburton I came to a little place called Dean and at the end of it ascended a very steep hill, all rock almost and so it was like so many steps up; this is called Dean Clapperhill, it was an untoward place but not soe formidable to me as the people of the place where I lay described it, haveing gone much worse

hills in the North; all along on the road where the lanes
are a little broader you ride by rowes of trees on each
side set and kept exactly even and cut, the tops being for
shade and beauty, and they in exact forme, as if a grove
to some house; at first I thought it was neer some houses,
till the frequency and length proved the contrary, for
there are very few if any houses neare the road, unless
the little villages you passe through; this country being
almost full of stone the streetes and roades too have a
naturall sort of paveing or pitching, tho' uneven; all their
carriages are here on the backs of horses with sort of
hookes like yoakes stands upon each side of a good
heigth, which are the receptacles of their goods, either
wood furse or lime or coal or corn or hay or straw, or
what else they convey from place to place; and I cannot
see how two such horses can pass each other or indeed
in some places how any horse can pass by each other,
and yet these are the roads that are all here abouts; some
little corners may jutt out that one may a little get out
of the way of each other, but this but seldom.

Two mile from Plymouth we come to the river Plym
just by a little town all built of stone and the tyleing is
all slatt, which with the lime its cemented with makes it
look white like snow, and in the sun shineing on the slatt
it glisters; here I came in sight on the right hand of a
very large house built all with this sort of stone which is
a sort of marble; even all quarryes are and some fine
marble this house look'd very finely in a thicket of trees
like a grove and was on the side of a hill, and led just
down to the head of the river Plym which is fill'd with
the tyde from the sea; and here I cross'd it on a stone

bridge, soe I rode 2 miles mostly by the river, which encreases and is a fine broad streame and at the town which is its mouth it falls into the sea; the sea here runs into severall creekes, one place it runs up to the Dock and Milbrook another arm of the sea goes up to Saltash and Port Eliot.

Plymouth is 2 Parishes called the old town and the new, the houses all built of this marble and the slatt at the top lookes like lead and glisters in the sun; there are noe great houses in the town; the streetes are good and clean, there is a great many tho' some are but narrow; they are mostly inhabitted with seamen and those which have affaires on the sea, for here up to the town there is a depth of water for shipps of the first rate to ride; its great sea and dangerous, by reason of the severall poynts of land between which the sea runs up a great way, and there are severall little islands alsoe, all which beares the severall tydes hard one against the other; there are two keyes the one is a broad space which leads you up into the broad streete and is used in manner of an exchange for the merchants meeteing, for in this streete alsoe is a fine stone Crosse and alsoe a long Market House set on stone pillars; there are severall good Cunduits to convey the water to the town, which conveyance the famous Sir Francis Drake (which did encompass the world in Queen Elizabeths days and landed safe at Plymouth) he gave this to the town; there are two Churches in the town but nothing fine; I was in the best and saw only King Charles the First Picture at length at prayer just as its cut on the frontispiece of the Irenicum, this picture was drawn and given the Church when he was in his troubles for some piece of service shown him; the alter stands in the Chancell or railed place, but it stands table wise the length and not up against the wall; the font was of marble and indeed soe is all buildings here, for their stone is all a sort of marble, some coarser, some finer; there are 4 large Meetings for the Descenters in the town takeing in the Quakers and Anabaptists.

The mouth of the river just at the town is a very good harbour for shipps; the Dock yards are about 2 mile from the town, by boate you goe to it the nearest way; its one of the best in England, a great many good shipps built there, and the great depth of water which comes up to it, tho' it runs up for 2 mile between the land, which also shelters the shipps; there is a great deale of buildings on the Dock, a very good house for the Masters and severall lesser ones and house for their cordage and makeing ropes, and all sorts of things required in building or refitting ships; it lookes like a little town the buildings are so many, and all of marble with fine slate on the rooffs, and at a little distance it makes all the houses shew as if they were cover'd with snow and glisters in the sunn which adds to their beauty.

The fine and only thing in Plymouth town is the Cittadell, or Castle, which stands very high above the town, the walls and battlements round it with all their works and plattforms are in very good repaire and lookes nobly, all marble full of towers with stone balls on the tops and gilt on the top, the entrance being by an ascent up a hill looks very noble over 2 drawbridges, and gates, which are marble, as is the whole well carv'd, the gate with armory and statues all gilt and on the top 7 gold

balls; the buildings within are very neate, a large appart-
ment for the Governour with others that are less for the
severall officers; there is a long building alsoe which is
the arsnell for the arms and amunition, and just by it a
round building well secured which was for the powder;
round the works is the plattform for the Gunns which
are well mounted and very well kept; walking round I
had the view of all the town and alsoe part off the main
Ocean, in which are some islands: there is St Nicholas
Island with a fort in it – there it was Harry Martin one
of the Kings Judges was banished dureing life – there
you can just discover a light house which is building on
a meer rock in the middle of the sea; this is 7 leagues off
it will be of great advantage for the guide of the shipps
that pass that way; from this you have a good refflection
on the great care and provision the wise God makes for
all persons and things in his Creation, that there should
be in some places, where there is any difficulty, rocks
even in the midst of the deep which can be made use of
for a constant guide and mark for the passengers on their
voyages; but the Earth is full of the goodness of the Lord
and soe is this Great Sea wherein are inumerable beings
created and preserv'd by the same Almighty hand, whose
is the Earth and all things there in, he is Lord of all.

From the plattform I could see the Dock and also just
against it I saw Mount Edgecomb a seate of Sir Richard
Edgcomes; it stands on the side of a hill all bedeck'd with
woods which are divided into severall rowes of trees in
walks, the house being all of this white marble; its built
round a Court so the four sides are alike, at the corners
of it are towers which with the Lanthorne or Cupilow

in the middle lookes well; the house is not very lofty nor the windows high but it looked like a very uniforme neate building and pretty large; there is a long walke from one part of the front down to the waterside, which is on a descent guarded with shady rowes of trees; there is a fine terrass walled in at the water side with open gates in the middle, and a sumer house at each end from whence a wall is drawn round the house and gardens, and a large parck the walls of which I rode by a good while; so that altogether and its scituation makes it esteemed by me the finest seat I have seen, and might be more rightly named Mount Pleasant.

From Plymouth I went 1 mile to Cribly [Cremyll] Ferry which is a very hazardous passage, by reason of 3 tydes meeting; had I known the Danger before I should not have been very willing to have gone it, not but this is the constant way all people goe, and saved severall miles rideing; I was at least an hour going over, it was about a mile but indeed in some places, notwithstanding there was 5 men row'd and I sett my own men to row alsoe I do believe we made not a step of way for almost a quarter of an hour, but blessed be God I came safely over; but those ferry boates are soe wet and then the sea and wind is allwayes cold to be upon, that I never faile to catch cold in a ferry-boate as I did this day, haveing 2 more ferrys to cross tho' none soe bad or halfe soe long as this; thence to Milbrooke 2 mile and went all along by the water and had the full view of the Dock-yards.

Here I entred into Cornwall and soe passed over many very steep stony hills tho' here I had some 2 or 3 miles of exceeding good way on the downs, and then I came

to the steep precipices great rocky hills; ever and anon I
came down to the sea and rode by its side on the sand,
then mounted up againe on the hills which carryed me
along mostly in sight of the South sea; sometymes I was
in lanes full of rowes of trees and then I came down a
very steep stony hill to Louu 13 mile, and here I cross'd
a little arme of the sea on a bridge of 14 arches; this is a
pretty bigg seaport, a great many little houses all of
stone, from whence I was to ascend a very stormy and
steep hill, much worse and 3 tymes as long as Dean
Clapper hill, and soe I continued up and down hill.

Here indeed I met with more inclosed ground and soe
had more lanes and a deeper clay road, which by the
raine the night before had made it very dirty and full of
water; in many places in the road there are many holes
and sloughs where ever there is clay ground, and when
by raines they are filled with water its difficult to shun
danger; here my horse was quite down in one of these
holes full of water but by the good hand of God's
Providence which has allwayes been with me ever a
present help in tyme of need, for giving him a good strap
he flounc'd up againe, tho' he had gotten quite down his
head and all; yet did retrieve his feete and gott cleer off
the place with me on his back.

Soe I came to Hoile [Fowey], 8 mile more, they are
very long miles the farther West, but you have the
pleasure of rideing as if in a grove in most places, the
regular rowes of trees on each side the roade as if it were
an entrance into some Gentlemans ground to his house,
the cut hedges and trees; at Hoile I ferryed over againe
cross an arme of the sea, here it was not broad but

exceeding deep, this is the South sea which runs into many little creekes for severall miles into the land, which is all the rivers they have; I observed this to be exceeding salt, and as green as ever I saw the sea when I have been a league or two out from the land, which shews it must be very deep and great tides; this Hoile is a narrow stony town the streetes very close, and as I descended a great steep into the town soe I ascended one off it up a stony long hill farre worse and full of shelves and rocks and 3 tymes as long as Dean Clapperhill, which I name because when I was there they would have frighted me with its terribleness as the most inaccessible place as ever was and none like it, and my opinion is that it was but one or two steps to other places forty steps, and them with more hazard than this of Dean Clapper.

Well to pass on I went over some little heath ground, but mostly lanes and those stony and dirty 3 mile and halfe to Parr, here I ferry'd over againe, not but when the tyde is out you may ford it; thence I went over the heath and commons by the tinn mines, 3 miles and halfe to St Austins [St Austell] which is a little Market town where I lay, but their houses are like barnes up to the top of the house; here was a pretty good dineing-roome and chamber within it, and very neate country women; my Landlady brought me one of the West Country tarts, this was the first I met with, though I had asked for them in many places in Sommerset and Devonshire, its an apple pye with a custard all on the top, its the most acceptable entertainment that could be made me; they scald their creame and milk in most parts of those countrys and so its a sort of clouted creame as we call it, with a little sugar, and soe put on the top of the apple pye; I was much pleased with my supper tho' not with the custome of the country, which is a universall smoaking both men women and children have all their pipes of tobacco in their mouths and soe sit round the fire smoaking, which was not delightfull to me when I went down to talke with my Landlady for information of any matter and customs amongst them; I must say they are as comely sort of women as I have seen any where tho' in ordinary dress, good black eyes and crafty enough and very neate.

Halfe a mile from hence they blow their tin which I went to see: they take the oar [ore] and pound it in a stamping mill which resembles the paper mills, and when its fine as the finest sand, some of which I saw and took, this they fling into a furnace and with it coale to make the fire, so it burns together and makes a violent heate and fierce flame, the mettle by the fire being seperated from the coale and its own drosse, being heavy falls down to a trench made to receive it, at the furnace hole below; this liquid mettle I saw them shovel up with an iron shovel and soe pour it into molds in which it cooles and soe they take it thence in sort of wedges or piggs I think they call them; its a fine mettle thus in its first melting looks like silver, I had a piece poured out and made cold for to take with me; the oare as its just dug lookes like the thunderstones, a greenish hue full of pin-dust; this seemes to containe its full description, the shineing part is white.

I went a mile farther on the hills and soe came where they were digging in the Tinn mines, there was at least

Celia Fiennes

20 mines all in sight which employs a great many people
at work, almost night and day, but constantly all and
every day includeing the Lords day which they are forced
to, to prevent their mines being overflowed with water;
more than 1000 men are taken up about them, few mines
but had then almost 20 men and boys attending it either
down in the mines digging and carrying the oare to the
little bucket which conveys it up, or else others are
draineing the water and looking to the engines that are
draineing it, and those above are attending the drawing up the oare in a sort of windless as is to a well; two
men keeps turning bringing up one and letting down
another, they are much like the leather buckets they use
in London to put out fire which hang up in churches and
great mens halls; they have a great labour and great
expence to draine the mines of the water with mills that
horses turn and now they have the mills or water engines
that are turned by the water, which is convey'd on
frames of timber and truncks to hold the water, which
falls down on the wheeles, as an over shott mill – and
these are the sort that turns the water into the severall
towns I have seen about London Darby and Exeter, and
many places more; they do five tymes more good than
the mills they use to turn with horses, but then they are
much more chargeable; those mines do require a great
deale of timber to support them and to make all these
engines and mills, which makes fewell very scarce here;
they burn mostly turffs which is an unpleasant smell, it
makes one smell as if smoaked like bacon; this oar as
said is made fine powder in a stamping mill which is like
the paper mills, only these are pounded drye and noe

water let into them as is to the raggs to work them into a paste; the mills are all turned with a little streame or channell of water you may step over; indeed they have noe other mills but such in all the country, I saw not a windmill all over Cornwall or Devonshire tho' they have wind and hills enough, and it may be its too bleake for them.

In the Tinn mines there is stone dug out and a sort of spar something like what I have seen in the Lead mines at Darbyshire but it seemed more sollid and hard it shines and lookes like mother of pearle; they alsoe digg out stones as cleer as Christal which is called Cornish Diamonds – I saw one as bigg as my two fists, very cleer and like some pieces of Chrystal my father brought from the Alps in Italy which I have got by me, I got one of those pieces of their Cornish Diamonds as long as halfe my finger, which had three or four flatt sides with edges, the top was sharpe and so hard as it would cut a letter on glass.

Thence I went to Tregna [Tregony], 6 miles good way, and passed by 100 mines, some on which they were at work, others that were lost by the waters overwhelming them; I crossed the water on a long stone bridge and so through dirty stony lanes 3 mile and then I came into a broad coach rode which I have not seen since I left Exeter; so I went 3 mile more to Mr Bescawens Trygoltny [Tregothnan] a Relation of mine; his house stands on a high hill in the middle of a parke with severall rows of trees with woods beyond it; the house is built all of white stone like the rough coarse marble and cover'd with slate; they use much lime in their cement which makes both walls and cover look very white; there is a Court walled round with open iron gates and barrs; the entrance is up a few stone steps into a large high hall and so to a passage that leads foreright up a good stair-case; on the right side is a large common parlour for constant eating in, from whence goes a little roome for smoking that has a back way into the kitchin, and on the left hand is a great parlour and drawing roome wanscoated all very well, but plaine, the great parlour is Cedar, out of that is the drawing-roome, which is hung with pictures of the family; that goes into the garden which has gravel walks round and across, but the squares are full of goosebery and shrub-trees and looks more like a kitchen garden as Lady Mary Bescawen told me, out of which is another garden and orchard which is something like a grove, green walks with rows of fruit trees; its capable of being a fine place with some charge, the roomes above are new modell'd, 3 roomes wanscoated and hung as the new way is, and the beds made up well, one red damaske, another green, another wrought, some of the Ladyes own work and well made up which is her own roome with a dressing-roome by it; there is a dressing roome and a roome for a servant just by the best chamber; there are two other good roomes nualter'd with old hangings to the bottom on wrought work of the first Ladyes Lady Margets work, that was my Cos'n German; within that roome was a servants roome and back stairs there was just such another apartment on the other side; between all from the stairs a broad passage leads to a Balcony over the entrance which look'd very pleasantly over the parke, but in the Cupulo on the Leads I could see a vast way at least 20 mile round, for this house stands very high to the land side; eastward and the south was the Great Ocean which runns into Falmouth thats the best harbour for shipps in that road; 6 mile from this place westward was to Truro, and the north to the hills full of Copper mines.

Here I was very civily entertained; from thence I returned back, intending not to go to the Lands End which was 30 miles farther, for feare of the raines that fell in the night which made me doubt what travelling I should have; soe to St Culomb I went a pretty long 12 mile; here I met with many rowes of elm trees which I have not found in any country except Wiltshire, these were mostly soe, tho' there were alsoe ashes and oakes; the hedges were hazelthorne and holly but to see soe many good rowes of trees on the road is surpriseing, and lookes like the entrance to some Gentlemans house, and I cannot tell but some of them were soe, tho' a mile off from the house.

The next day finding it faire weather on the change of the moone I alter'd my resolution, and soe went for the Lands End by Redruth 18 mile mostly over heath and downs which was very bleake and full of mines; here I came by the Copper mines, which have the same order in the digging and draining tho' here it seemes dryer and I believe not quite soe annoy'd with water; the oar is something as the tinn only this looks blackish or rather a purple colour and the glistering part is yellow as the other was white; they do not melt it here but ship it off to Bristol by the North Sea, which I rode in sight of, and is not above 2 or 3 mile from hence; which supplyes them with coales for their fewell at easyer rates than the other side, Plymouth and the South Sea, because since the warre they could not double the poynt at the Lands End being so neer France, the pirats or privateers met them; indeed at St Ives they do melt a little but nothing that is considerable, thats 10 mile from Redruth which is a little Market town; here they carry all their things on horses backs, soe that of a market day which was Fryday you see a great number of horses little of size which they call Cornish Canelys; they are well made and strong and will trip along as light on the stony road without injury to themselves, whereas my horses went so heavy that they wore their shoes immediately thinn and off – but here I met with a very good smith that shooed the horses as well as they do in London, and that is not common in the country, but here I found it soe and at a place in Westmoreland by the fells a smith made good shoes and set them on very well.

From Redruth I went to Pensands 15 mile, and passed by the ruines of great fortification or Castle on a high hill about 3 mile from Redruth and passed to Haile, and soe went by the sea side a great way, it being spring tide it was a full sea; just over against it there was a Church which was almost sunck into the sands being a very sandy place, so I went up pretty high hills and over some heath or common, on which a great storme of haile and raine met me, and drove fiercely on me but the wind soone dry'd my dust coate; here I came by a very good grove of trees which I thought was by some Gentlemans house, but found it some farmers.

The people here are very ill guides, and know but

little from home, only to some market town they frequent, but will be very solicitous to know where you goe, and how farre, and from whence you came, and where is the abode; then I came in sight of the hill in Cornwall called the Mount [St Michael's Mount] its on a rock in the sea which at the flowing tyde is an island but at low water one can goe over the sands almost just to it; but a little way from Market Due [Marazion] a little market town which is about 2 mile from Penzants and you may walke or ride to it all on the sands when the tyde's out; its a fine rock, and very high, severall little houses for fisher men in the sides of it just by the water; at the top is a pretty good house where the Govenour lives sometymes, Sir Hook his name is; there is a tower on the top on which is a flag; there is a chaire or throne on the top from whence they can discover a great way at sea and here they put up Lights to direct shipps.

Pensands is rightly named being all sands about it; it lies just as a shore to the maine south ocean which comes from the Lizard, and being on the side of a hill with a high hill all round the side to the landward, it lookes soe snugg and warme and truely it needs shelter haveing the sea on the other side and little or no fewell; turff and furse and ferne; they have little or noe wood and noe coale which differences it from Darbyshire, otherwise this and to the Lands End is stone and barren as Darbyshire; I was surprised to find my supper boyling on a fire allwayes supply'd with a bush of furse and that to be the only fewell to dress a joynt of meat and broth, and told them they could not roast me anything, but they have a little wood for such occasions but its scarce and dear – which is a strange thing that the shipps should not supply them, they told me it must be all brought round the Land End, and since the warre they could not have it – this town is two parishes, one Church in the town and a little Chapple, and another Church belonging to the other parish which is a mile distance, there is alsoe a good Meeteing place.

There is a good Key and a good Harbour for the shipps to ride, by meanes of the point of land which runns into the sea in a neck or compass which shelters it from the maine, and answers the Lizard Point which you see very plaine, a point of land looks like a double hill one above the other that runns a good way into the sea; the Lands End is 10 mile farther, pretty good way but much up hills and down, pretty steep and narrow lanes, but its not shelter'd with trees or hedg rows this being rather desart and like the Peake Country in Darbyshire, dry stone walls and the hills full of stones; but it is in most places better land and yeilds good corne both wheate barley and oates and some rhye; about 2 mile from the Lands End I came in sight of the maine ocean on both sides, the south and north sea, and soe rode in its view till I saw them joyn'd at the poynt, and saw the Island of Sily which is 7 leagues off the Lands End; they tell me that in a cleer day those in the Island can discern the people on the maine as they goe up the hill to Church, they can describe their clothes; this Church and little parish which is called Church town is about a mile from the poynt, the houses are but poor cottages like barns to look on, much like those in Scotland – but to doe my own Country its right the inside of their little cottages are clean and plaister'd, and such as you might comfortably eate and drink there, and for curiosity sake I dranck there, and met with very good bottled ale.

The Lands End terminates in a poynt or peak of great rocks which runs a good way into the sea, I clamber'd over them as farre as safety permitted me; there are abundance of rocks and sholes of stones stands up in the sea, a mile off some, and soe here and there some quite to the shore, which they name by severall names of Knights and Ladies roled up in mantles from some old tradition or fiction the poets advance, description of the amours of some great persons, but these many rocks and stones which lookes like the Needles in the Isle of Wight makes it hazardous for shipps to double the poynt especially in stormy weather; here at the Lands End they are but a little way off of France 2 days saile at farthest convey them to Haure De Grace in France, but the peace being but newly entred into with the French I was not willing to venture, at least by my self, into a Forreign Kingdom, and being then at the end of the land my horses leggs could not carry me through the deep and so return'd againe to Pensands 10 mile more, and soe came in view of both the seas and saw the Lizard Point and Pensands, the Mount in Cornwall which looked very fine in the broad day the sunn shineing on the rocke in the sea.

THE STORY OF PENGUIN CLASSICS

Before 1946 …'Classics' are mainly the domain of academics and students, without readable editions for everyone else. This all changes when a little-known classicist, E. V. Rieu, presents Penguin founder Allen Lane with the translation of Homer's Odyssey that he has been working on and reading to his wife Nelly in his spare time.

1946 The Odyssey becomes the first Penguin Classic published, and promptly sells three million copies. Suddenly, classic books are no longer for the privileged few.

1950s Rieu, now series editor, turns to professional writers for the best modern, readable translations, including Dorothy L. Sayers's *Inferno* and Robert Graves's *The Twelve Caesars*, which revives the salacious original.

1960s 1961 sees the arrival of the Penguin Modern Classics, showcasing the best twentieth-century writers from around the world. Rieu retires in 1964, hailing the Penguin Classics list as 'the greatest educative force of the 20th century'.

1970s A new generation of translators arrives to swell the Penguin Classics ranks, and the list grows to encompass more philosophy, religion, science, history and politics.

1980s The Penguin American Library joins the Classics stable, with titles such as *The Last of the Mohicans* safeguarded. Penguin Classics now offers the most comprehensive library of world literature available.

1990s Penguin Popular Classics are launched, offering readers budget editions of the greatest works of literature. Penguin Audiobooks brings the classics to a listening audience for the first time, and in 1999 the launch of the Penguin Classics website takes them online to an ever larger global readership.

The 21st Century Penguin Classics are rejacketed for the first time in nearly twenty years. This world famous series now consists of more than 1,300 titles, making the widest range of the best books ever written available to millions – and constantly redefining the meaning of what makes a 'classic'.

The Odyssey continues …

The best books ever written

PENGUIN (🐧) CLASSICS

SINCE 1946